The FAITH *of the* PRESIDENTS

OUR NATIONAL LEADERS AT PRAYER

RON DiCIANNI

Charisma
HOUSE
A STRANG COMPANY

Most STRANG COMMUNICATIONS/CHARISMA HOUSE/SILOAM products
are available at special quantity discounts for bulk purchase for sales
promotions, premiums, fund-raising, and educational needs. For details,
write Strang Communications/Charisma House/Siloam, 600 Rinehart
Road, Lake Mary, Florida 32746, or telephone (407) 333-0600.

THE FAITH OF THE PRESIDENTS by Ron DiCianni
Published by Charisma House
A Strang Company
600 Rinehart Road
Lake Mary, Florida 32746
www.charismahouse.com

Unless otherwise noted, all Scripture quotations are from the King
James Version of the Bible.

Cover illustration copyright © by Ron DiCianni
Black and white graphics of the presidents
used by permission of Bartleby.com, Inc.

Cover design by Joe De Leon
Interior design and typography by Terry Clifton

Library of Congress Cataloging-in-Publication Data
DiCianni, Ron.
The faith of the presidents / Ron DiCianni.
    p. cm.
Includes bibliographical references.
ISBN 1-59185-467-9 (hardback)
1. Presidents--United States--Biography. 2. Presidents--United
States--Religion. 3. United States--Politics and government--Case
studies. 4. Christianity and politics--United States--Case studies. I.
Title.
E176.1.D525 2004
973'.09'9--dc22
                                            2004008665

04 05 06 07 08 — 987654321

DEDICATION

$\mathcal{I}$ acknowledge the privilege that is mine to be called a Christ follower. To Jesus Christ alone do I bow in recognition that He is Lord.

Every author needs help from a good assistant. Mine came from the best. Not only a skilled researcher and writer, but far more to me as my son, I proudly give my thanks to you, Grant. In you, God gave me a skilled craftsman, as found in the temple artisans in the Book of Exodus. Your skill is with words, and a fine wordsmith you are! You held my arms up when they were tired, just as Aaron and Hur did for Moses. I thank God for you.

Love,
Dad

ACKNOWLEDGMENTS

- As always to the Lord Jesus Christ, whose sacrifice and blessing gives us something worth writing and painting about.

- Our editor, Lillian McAnally, and all the great people at Strang Communications Company—especially our longtime family friend Barbara Dycus for giving the book a great new direction.

- With inexpressible thanks to those who have fought and continue to fight even now to allow people to sit and write books. Your sacrifice has continued to defend our freedom.

- Finally, to the leaders of this country who continue to remember that they need God. I pray we never see the day when a president feels that he is able to govern on his own.

CONTENTS

INTRODUCTION

The United States of America has become morally and spiritually adrift from its foundational principles. Proof of this statement lies within America's everyday life. Newspapers, magazines, and even children's cartoons point to a country that has become a sea of immorality. The only good news is that America still has a nucleus of people who pray to God and have faith in Him.

What makes America different as a nation is our Judeo-Christian heritage. Granted, many might argue with that last statement. The new trend in countercultural thinking is that everything is relative, and to base a governmental system on religion is lunacy because there are no absolutes. Regardless of the resolution to that argument, our nation's history has volumes to say on the subject of faith and government. Before looking at the spiritual life of individual leaders, it is imperative to examine the choice and statements made by our early government. The choices that early leaders made resoundingly point to their priorities and outline what they held most dear. In the case of our founding fathers, God and their personal spiritual beliefs were significantly important not only in their own lives, but also in governing the nation.

One of the documents that forged our nation, the Declaration of Independence, points to God as one of the central themes and refers to God in four separate sections. He is referred to as the "Creator of man," the "God of Nature," "Divine Providence," and the "Supreme Judge of the world." It would seem, then, that those men who founded this country placed a high value on their faith. In this political document, God and His laws are argued as the justification for the colonies' decision to declare independence. Not only did our Founding Fathers see a direct correlation between religion and state, but they also saw the two as inseparable.

Under the assumption that someone could argue away the meaningfulness of these references to God as simple consensus building or else a concession to an ultrareligious faction among the Founding Fathers, let's examine the actions of our Congress. One of the early acts of both the House and the Senate was to independently approve the appointment of a chaplain for each body. In addition, each chaplain was to draw a salary from the still struggling federal budget. As if this wasn't proof enough, Congress declared that each session was to be opened and closed with prayer. And that has continued right through the turn of the millennium. Congress has had thousands of members throughout the decades, but each session has been blessed by prayer. The newly formed Congress directed two other very significant actions to honor the Christian heritage upon which they were building the nation. In 1789, they unanimously approved a measure directing President George Washington to "declare a day of Thanksgiving and prayer" for the specific purpose of allowing the public to reflect on "the many signal favors of God, especially by affording them an opportunity peaceably to establish a constitution of government." Last, as an everlasting reminder, the design of our currency, mandated and approved by Congress, includes the phrase "In God We Trust" prominently displayed on every bill and coin minted. Certainly the burgeoning Congress, the "people's" representatives in government, considered God to be an integral part of public, private, and governmental policy.

The course of our nation's history has helped this book

to write itself. From General George Washington's famous "prayer at Valley Forge" to President George W. Bush's prayer at a podium during America's terrorist crises, it becomes clear that prayer has been the mighty refuge of our presidents.

Chronicling the faith of presidents through their words has put back into perspective our nation's dependency upon God Almighty.

Whether in days of peace and prosperity, or in the desperate days of war and national crisis, history records that we are a Christian nation. We may change the future, but we cannot change the past.

Regardless of what you may personally believe or what you have been taught, here it is for the record—the faith of our presidents knit together to form an address called "prayer."

The prayers differ, of course. The Listener is always the same.

As you read the words of each president, imagine yourself being there at that moment in time. Stop to reflect on what struggles must have burdened the hearts of these men who, at times, carried the "weight of the world on their shoulders." Ponder their great need for direction beyond human wisdom, with such matters at stake that would make the strongest of men shudder.

Alexis de Tocqueville, a French statesman and theorist who came to America in the 1830s, in part answered the question, "What makes America great?" His conclusions spanned hundreds of pages and were published in two separate volumes. Time and again Alexis de Tocqueville referred back to America's religious heritage as a primary reason for her success. He, in fact, remarked that the first thing that struck him was the "religious aspect" of the new country and that the longer he stayed, the more he saw how faith and government were intertwined. Although he came to many theories on the relation between faith and the American government, these two quotes provide a glimpse into his conclusion:

> [T]here is no country in the world where the Christian religion retains a greater influence over the souls of men than in America, and there can be no greater proof of its utility and of its conformity to human nature than that its influence is powerfully felt over the most enlightened and free nation of the earth.
>
> Not until I went into the churches of America and heard her pulpits flame with righteousness did I understand the secret of her genius and power.

Alexis de Tocqueville was possibly one of the best minds of his generation. Still today, his work in various social fields remains required reading. How fitting it is that the independent confirmation of America's spiritual heritage comes from such a source.

Early America and Christianity were inseparable. This nation's founders and architects clearly left a spiritual heritage for later generations to follow. Our presidents have wisely and universally embraced, and continued, that heritage. Although every man is fallible and not all of our leaders were "perfect" role models, the fact remains that the results of their faith and prayers should be an encouragement to us in good times and bad.

In the final analysis, faith and prayer are still alive and well. The more we seek God's wisdom, the more God will grant the adage in troubled times, "God Bless America."

—RON DiCIANNI

In regard to the personal lives of certain presidents, while we as Christians do not condone any questionable and morally suspect actions, we should choose not to use them as the basis of a conclusion against the men who made them. Man is a fallen creature, and each one of us has made decisions that, to some extent, may call into question our fitness to proclaim our Christianity. While some of these men may have failed, we believe absolutely that Jesus' death is sufficient to grant forgiveness for any act to anyone who asks for it. Each of the presidents in question publicly or privately acknowledged regret for their actions, and we must leave the decision of their fate up to God. This book only seeks to show that even those presidents whose conduct was questionable still found it essential to appear in the presence of the Almighty on bended knee and ask direction for the nation. They say that there are no atheists in foxholes. Likewise, the same axiom holds true for those individuals who find themselves in the heat of battle in the White House.

GEORGE WASHINGTON

Born: February 22, 1732, in
Westmoreland County, Virginia

★ ★ ★ ★

PRESIDENT: 1789-1797

A young man, barely twenty, sits down before a writing table. The candlelight is only a flicker in this Sunday pre-dawn gray. With a flourish of his quill, he pens these words into his prayer journal:

> I beseech thee, my sins, remove them from thy presence, as far as the east is from the west, and accept of me for the merits of thy Son, Jesus Christ, that when I come into thy temple, and compass thine altar, my prayers may come before thee as incense; and as thou wouldst hear me calling upon thee in my prayers, so give me grace to hear thee calling on me in thy word, that it may be wisdom, righteousness, reconciliation and peace to the saving of the soul in the day of the Lord Jesus. Grant that I may hear it with reverence, receive it with meekness, mingle it with faith, and that it may accomplish in me, Gracious God, the good work for which thou has sent it.

A general and the first president of a new republic, the United States of America, George Washington has been a source of fascination since 1778. It is important to realize that Washington was not predisposed by status toward challenging British rule. As the son of a propertied family, Washington was positioned for a comfortable life of local power and prestige. In fact, one of his first adventures as a teenager was to help map and survey the area of Shenandoah for Lord Fairfax.

The life that Washington could expect was one typical of eighteenth-century Virginia. He would be an area gentleman, manage his land, and engage in commerce. Many men in Washington's social class would become involved in local governance or the military, and he was no exception. As an officer, Washington won acclaim in the Seven Years' War and would bring that experience to bear as he led his rag-tag collection of troops on to defeat the mightiest army of the time during the Revolutionary War. Lest one think he avoided the front lines, George Washington's coat was pierced by four bullets, and his horse was shot twice during one encounter in 1755. But Washington emerged uninjured.

Bless, O Lord, all the people of this land, from the highest to the lowest, particularly those whom thou has appointed to rule over us in church and state.

Much of today's national attitudes and policies were enacted by or under Washington. Indeed, he set the tenor for the American system of governance. His greatest fear, however, was that the ideals upon which the new nation was founded would give way to the demands of ideology and petty squabbling. To that end, Washington was careful to respect the powers and rights given to Congress and to the individual states under the Constitution. Struggling with the growing pains of a new nation and foreign tensions with the French and English, Washington was exploring vastly uncharted territory. His compensation for that struggle was $25,000 per year. It was, however, a concerned leader who stepped down after a second term. President Washington commented that his greatest worry for the American people was that the government would fracture along ideological and political lines to the detriment of the nation. The American government envisioned by George Washington was much different in spirit than the political climate of today.

✶ ✶ HIS LEGACY ✶ ✶

Beyond his public acclaim, Washington was a man of intense faith. As an elder in his church for almost twenty years, Washington always made God a priority. Many of those around him remarked on the sincerity of the first president's faith in their own journals. Washington was recorded by Henry Cabot Lodge to be a Christian of "simple and childlike faith" with "no doubts or questionings but believ[ing] always in an overruling providence and in a merciful God." Washington carried these cherished beliefs to the highest office of the land where he proclaimed that it was his desire for the government's actions to be fixed on "true principles." George Washington was a president of many "firsts" for America. He was the first five-star general (awarded posthumously), the first president, the first commander in chief, and one of the Founding Fathers of this nation. The words of his farewell address ring as true today as when he proclaimed, "Reason and experience both forbid us to expect that national morality can exist apart from religious principle."

Years later, a seasoned statesman and leader of the newly formed America recalls his Christian heritage as he proclaims the first Thanksgiving:

> Now, therefore, I do recommend and assign Thursday, the 26th day of November next, to be devoted by the people of these States to the service of that great and glorious Being who is the beneficent author of all the good that was, that is, or that will be; that we may then all unite in rendering unto Him our sincere and humble thanks for His kind care and protection of the people of this country previous to their becoming a nation; for the signal and manifold mercies and the favorable interpositions of His providence in the course and conclusion of the late war; for the great degree of tranquility, union, and plenty which we have since enjoyed; for the peaceable and rational manner in which we have been enabled to establish constitutions of government for our safety and happiness, and particularly the national one now lately instituted for the civil and religious liberty with which we are blessed, and the means we have of acquiring and diffusing useful knowledge; and, in general, for all the great and various favors which He has been pleased to confer upon us.
>
> —OCTOBER 3, 1789

This statement was part of George Washington's Thanksgiving Proclamation establishing November 26, 1789 as a day of national thanksgiving and prayer as requested by a unanimous vote of Congress. Although a day of thanksgiving had been celebrated before and after his presidency, Washington's proclamation represents the first one by the newly formed government.

✶ ✶ HIS FAITH ✶ ✶

Picture a man wearing a white wig standing on a balcony before a multitude of spectators. A cool April wind blows through the square in New York. America's first president asks for a Bible and humbly utters the first words of a new presidency. Little does the crowd below know that these words—"so help me God"—are Washington's own addition to the oath of office. Once again this famous leader has set a precedent for those who follow.

From his first day as president, Washington was un-ashamed to publicly express his faith and need for God. As the leader of a new nation stepping into uncharted territory, Washington had to be endowed with great faith in God. Developing "childlike faith" like that of George Washington's results from constant prayer and the realization that we can do nothing apart from the Father.

Perhaps you realize that it is time to shift the focus of your faith from people or things, and turn it toward the only One who can help you when you face monumental decisions.

✳ ✳ FAITH IN ACTION ✳ ✳

Lord, grant me this day the wisdom to heed Your Word. I know that I am a sinner, but by Your grace You saved me. I pray that You watch over my family and me and that Your hand guides us each day. Help me to obey those in authority over me, and let me live my life in service to You showing Your salvation to those around me regardless of their race or social position. Amen.

JOHN ADAMS

Born: October 30, 1735,
in Braintree, Massachusetts

⋆ ⋆ ⋆ ⋆

PRESIDENT: 1797–1801

*P*rior to his inauguration, John Adams dedicated his new home to God. This private residence of the second president of the United States, and of every president to succeed him, would become a national monument—the White House. In a damp, unfinished room of the White House, John Adams penned these words in a letter to his wife, Abigail, on his second night in the new house:

> I pray heaven to bestow the best of blessings on this house and on all that shall hereafter inhabit it. May none but honest and wise men ever rule under this roof!

—NOVEMBER 2, 1800

⋆ ⋆ HIS LIFE ⋆ ⋆

*J*ohn Adams, the country's second president, faced a slightly different landscape than did his predecessor. Although still a trailblazer in what it meant to be president, Adams, as many believed, was more of a theorist and philosopher than a politician. Adams was vice president under Washington and was eager to make a more significant contribution leaving behind what he considered a poorly suited and insignificant post. As an early patriot, John Adams used his law degree from Harvard to contribute to the success of independence as a delegate to both the first and second Continental Congress. Born in 1735 and president from 1797–1801, Adams faced a growing rift in the American political consciousness. Instead of a united front against a common enemy, Americans were splitting along the ideology of the separate parties, just as Washington had feared. Adams's most vocal critics were the Hamiltonians, named after the architect of the Bank of the United States, Alexander Hamilton. Since Adams was one of the founders of the Federalist Party, this animosity with the Hamiltonians was what would influence the next election against Adams.

✯ ✯ HIS LEGACY ✯ ✯

*U*nder John Adams, the nation moved forward in international acknowledgment. A brief war with the French and the development of American naval prowess went a long way in pushing America to the front ranks of the global landscape. One great achievement of his presidency was the successful completion of the new presidential residence, now called the White House, which Adams occupied in November of 1800, before it was even fully furnished.

> *It must be felt that there is no national security but in the nation's humble acknowledged dependence upon God and His overruling providence.*

The end of Adams's presidency came about at the hands of his rival and vice president, Thomas Jefferson. Shortly before the 1800 election, Adams had decided that reopening negotiations with France was in his country's best interest, but a majority of his party disagreed, which caused a split in his support. Although it was the act that sealed his defeat, negotiating peace with France was, according to Adams, one of the most successful acts of his term. Amazingly, on his deathbed, Adams's last words would be that Jefferson had outlived him. In fact, and unknown to Adams, Thomas Jefferson had died just a few hours before John Adams.

✷ ✷ HIS FAITH ✷ ✷

*Y*ears before assuming the presidency, a youthful Adams sits under a tree basking in the cool spring air in reflective thought and then scratches this statement of logic and faith into his school journal:

> The great and Almighty author of nature, who at first established those rules which regulate the world, can as easily suspend those laws whenever his providence sees sufficient reason for such suspension. This can be no objection, then, to the miracles of Jesus Christ.
>
> —MARCH 2, 1756

As a Christian, Adams believed that freedom and Christianity were intricately linked. To be a Christian nation was to be a free nation. Adams pointed to the New Testament as his source for those beliefs. Many sources show that Adams encouraged his fellow colonists to discuss and debate these "Christian" principles openly in the common marketplace. It was John Adams who suggested that the first Continental Congress be opened in prayer. Most interestingly is a book of poetry Adams wrote, which frequently includes poems to and about Jesus and Christianity.

Adams did not shy away from proclaiming his faith in God and his belief that prayer should precede political decision making.

How much more do we need to pray for faith to take a stand for those values that God has placed before us in His Word. We also need to pray for the leadership of this nation, which God's Word commands us to do.

☆ ☆ FAITH IN ACTION ☆ ☆

Lord, I acknowledge that there is no safety save the protection found in You. I pray for those who step foot in this house that they see You reflected in my life. You are the Author of all creation, and there is nothing You cannot do if I will only trust You. Let me believe and glory in the miracles of Your Son and His ultimate sacrifice. Amen.

THOMAS JEFFERSON

*Born: April 13, 1743,
in Albermarle County, Virginia*

★ ★ ★ ★

PRESIDENT: 1801–1809

With a flourish of his pen and a decisive look of defiance, Jefferson bends to the portable desk balanced on his knees and intertwines these words of faith into one of the most powerful documents ever crafted by human hands:

> We hold these truths to be self evident, that all men are created equal, that they are endowed by their Creator with certain unalienable Rights....We, therefore, the Representatives of the united States of America, in General Congress, Assembled, appealing to the Supreme Judge of the world for the rectitude of our intentions....And for the support of this Declaration, with a firm reliance on the protection of divine Providence, we mutually pledge to each other our Lives, our Fortunes, and our sacred Honor.
>
> —DECLARATION OF INDEPENDENCE,
> ADOPTED JULY 4, 1776

✶ ✶ HIS LIFE ✶ ✶

Thomas Jefferson is probably one of the best-known and most influential founders of America. By far, his strongest suit was his writing ability, and this writing ability propelled him to fundamental greatness by penning the Declaration of Independence.

Born in 1743, Jefferson was the son of a landowner and enjoyed the advantage of a mother whose high social standing brought him quickly into circles that might have otherwise been unavailable. Trained as a lawyer, Jefferson wrote prolifically on several topics, and many of his writings have application beyond government or political application.

Following his term, Jefferson retired to his estate at Monticello, where he died just hours before his rival Adams. Amazingly, they both died on the day Americans celebrate their independence: July 4, 1826.

✶ ✶ HIS LEGACY ✶ ✶

Jefferson had a rocky start in government service. As Secretary of State under Washington, Jefferson resigned when his attitudes on independence evidenced sympathies toward the French, who were embroiled in a revolution of their own, and landed him in open conflict with Hamilton and other key officials. Differences with Hamilton finally pushed Jefferson into organizing his own political party with James Madison, called the Republicans.* During the presidency of his political rival, Adams, Jefferson served as vice president and later succeeded in beating him in the next election.

---

* Editor's note: The Republicans as formed by Jefferson are not the predecessors of the modern Republican Party. In fact many of the views espoused by Jefferson's party are often more in line with the modern Democratic Party. The modern-day Republican Party began circa 1850.

Jefferson's election was interesting on several fronts. Originally a candidate in the 1796 election, Jefferson came in second to Adams and, due to a flaw in the election process, became the vice president. The election of 1800 actually resulted in a tie, and Jefferson was chosen by the House of Representatives. Most notably, Jefferson's election surprised many internationally because it firmly established the concept of a two-party system in America and showed the world that power could be justly transferred between parties without bloodshed.

Although Jefferson was well acquainted with high society, he cared little for social graces or ideas of rank and status. His goal was a government run by simplicity and economic thrift. One great accomplishment of his presidency was the Louisiana Purchase, which added more than three-quarters of a million acres to the United States, effectively doubling the country.

...all men are created equal, that they are endowed by their Creator with certain unalienable Rights, that among these are Life, Liberty and the pursuit of Happiness.

—*Declaration of Independence*

Foreign policy was harder, though. After charting a failed course of neutrality between warring parties in Europe,

Jefferson focused on paying down the national debt and instituting economic policies to bolster the domestic health of the country.

As in many times before, the United States occupies a tenuous position in the world. A strong president, ever mindful of the dangers, stands before a throng of elected officials and, relying on the omnipotence of God, prays:

Almighty God, Who has given us this good land for our heritage: We humbly beseech Thee that we may always prove ourselves a people mindful of Thy favor and glad to do Thy will. Bless our land with honorable ministry, sound learning, and pure manners. Save us from violence, discord, and confusion, from pride and arrogance and from every evil way. Defend our liberties, and fashion into one united people the multitude brought hither out of many kindreds and tongues. Endow with Thy spirit wisdom those whom in Thy Name we entrust the authority of government, that there may be justice and peace at home, and that through obedience to Thy law, we may show forth Thy praise among the nations of earth. In time of prosperity fill our hearts with thankfulness, and in the day of trouble, suffer not our trust in Thee to fail; all of which we ask through Jesus Christ our Lord, amen.

—NATIONAL PRAYER FOR PEACE,
MARCH 4, 1805

Jefferson believed that faith and freedom were inseparable. He believed that it was every individual's "inalienable right" to pursue life, liberty, and happiness, and to have the freedom to worship God and exercise his or her faith as the person so chooses.

✭ ✭ HIS FAITH ✭ ✭

If we knew nothing else of Jefferson beyond what he had written in the Declaration of Independence, it would seem those words were enough to bring to light his intense faith. By acknowledging a Creator who had guided his life and instilled in Americans the very liberties that they were prepared to fight for, Jefferson boldly proclaimed his Christian beliefs.

Perhaps the most well-known and misconstrued Jeffersonian phrase is, "wall of separation between church and state," which has come to represent all that Jefferson opposed. As a man of faith, Jefferson believed in protecting every individual's religious freedom without the establishment of a government-recognized church, such as the one in the mother country, England. Jefferson wrote a bill establishing religious freedom, which was en acted in 1786.

May we, as an American nation, never take for granted our liberty, especially our freedom to worship.

✯ ✯ FAITH IN ACTION ✯ ✯

Thank You, Lord, that we live in a free nation, unopposed by the bonds of religious oppression. Fill our hearts with thankfulness, and in trials let us not waiver in our love for You. We praise You for indwelling us with freedom. Help us to strive to prove our devotion to You. Defend our liberties, and let us be a nation united unto You. We ask this in the name of our Lord Jesus Christ, amen.

JAMES MADISON

Born: March 16, 1751,
in Port Conway, Virginia

★ ★ ★ ★

PRESIDENT: 1809–1817

*M*any years before his election, James Madison makes the following argument against critics who seek to limit religion through their regulations. In a crowded meeting hall, he thunders these words to the assembled leaders:

> Before any man can be considered a member of civil society, he must be considered as a subject of the Governor of the Universe.
> —MEMORIAL AND REMONSTRANCE AGAINST RELIGIOUS ASSESSMENTS, JUNE 1785

★ ★ HIS LIFE ★ ★

*I*n the early to mid-1600s, Madison's family was considered a frontier family that settled in what would later become Virginia. James Madison grew up on a rather large tobacco plantation in Virginia. His family eventually acquired land and wealth as the surrounding area became more populated. His education included theology, languages, and Enlightenment literature. At the conclusion of his schooling at the College of New Jersey, Madison considered a career in law or becoming a pastor, but instead he chose to enter local government.

Madison married a younger woman, Dolly Payne Todd, when he was in his forties. Although she was raised in the Quaker Society, she would become known for her social graces and entertainment. She would outlive her husband by almost a decade. At the time of his death, Madison was actually the last of the Founding Fathers.

In Madison's day the title "Commander and Chief" was quite literally as it sounded, and Madison spent several days leading his troops on horseback as they dodged artillery fire in an attempt to escape the British attacks.

☆ ☆ HIS LEGACY ☆ ☆

It might seem odd, but James Madison's greatest contribution was not in being the nation's fourth president. During his life and throughout history, Madison, as many would argue, was in fact the "Father of the Constitution." He protested that title, however, and argued that the document was in fact "the work of many heads and many hands."

Madison's presidency saw some of the greatest upheaval and most significant events that the young country had ever witnessed. Often at the mercy of forces beyond his control, Madison would be at the nation's helm through political, national, and military hardships.

We have all been encouraged to feel the guardianship, and guidance of that Almighty Being, whose power regulates the destiny of nations.
    —Inaugural Address, March 4, 1809

Nevertheless, Madison, with Jefferson, was the driving force behind the creation of the Republican Party. It was that party whose supremacy was heightened by Madison's presidency. Despite great discord within the Republican Party, with Madison siding with the losing ideology in regard to the nation's future, he was still reelected. The win, in turn, was the death knell for his rivals, the Federalists. Although the future looked rosy on the political side, strong pressures both internal and external abounded.

On the international front, Madison confronted an uncertain and changing world. Napoleon Bonaparte had come on the scene in Europe. French and British warships continued to ruin sea commerce. Some saw the British aggression as proof that England had never really relinquished its claim on the colonies that had beaten it years before. Those confrontations, aggravated by unsuccessful attempts to retaliate on the sea, led to the War of 1812. During that war, the British invaded the northern United States, advancing as far south as Washington DC. In the process they burned the Capitol, the White House, and other public buildings. Yet, out of the ashes arose the star of the war: Lieutenant (three-star) General Andrew Jackson, who succeeded in halting the advance and driving the British out of the country.

Madison's last years in office were spent recovering from the damage of the war with the British and the political fallout of the Federalists. He was aided by a thriving new sense of pride and nationalism after defeating the world's strongest power for the second time.

Madison continued to use his brilliance to counteract what he saw as divisive and ruinous influences that he worried were destined to shatter the Republic. He retired to his property in Virginia, where he died almost two decades after leaving office.

James Madison took an interesting stand on faith. Certainly American history is wrought with differences between various denominations, but Madison rejected those differences. Once while visiting a local jail, he was appalled to find that Baptist ministers had been arrested because they were Baptist. His view was that each should be free to worship "God All Powerful Wise and Good" in their own fashion.

Challenged by his critics to reconcile his faith against his government, Madison made the following claim:

> We've staked the whole future of American civilization not on the power of government, far from it. We have staked the future of all our political institutions upon the capacity of each and all of us…to govern ourselves according to the commandments of God. The future and success of America is not in this Constitution, but in the laws of God upon which this Constitution is founded.

May our faith remain steadfast in what God can do through us and not in our own abilities.

✱ ✱ FAITH IN ACTION ✱ ✱

Father, every day is built on the foundation of Your love and power, not on our own abilities. Let me be a follower of Your Son, first and foremost, and help me to place everything else secondary. My success and destiny lie in Your will for my life. Help me to heed Your voice each day. Amen.

JAMES MONROE

Born: April 28, 1758,
in Westmoreland County, Virginia

★ ★ ★ ★

PRESIDENT: 1817–1825

*A*fter serving one term in office, Monroe is in the same place, before many of the same people. Addressing the crowd, he reminds the assembled leaders and himself where his strength lies:

> With a firm reliance on the protection of Almighty God, I shall forthwith commence the duties of the high trust to which you have called me.
> —SECOND INAUGURAL ADDRESS,
> MARCH 5, 1821

★ ★ HIS LIFE ★ ★

*M*onroe was born to a moderately prosperous land-owning family in Virginia. Like many people during that time, Monroe was an Episcopalian and certainly practiced those convictions in his everyday life. Thomas Jefferson once commented that Monroe was so honest that one could turn Monroe's soul inside out and still not find a speck of dirt. Prior to the presidency, Monroe had a life similar to those before him. He went to the College of William and Mary, after which he practiced law in Virginia. His education at William and Mary was cut short because he elected to join the Third Virginia Regiment in 1776. Frustrated by his inability to get a command after performing well in action, Monroe left the army in 1780 and turned to the study of law. It was there that he met and studied under Thomas Jefferson, who would become friend, mentor, and influential helper for this future president. In fact, in the late 1780s Monroe and his wife moved to be closer to Jefferson. Monroe's wife was considered one of the most beautiful women, yet she was formal and icily reserved. She did give him three children, but one of them, their only son, died very early.

✯ ✯ HIS LEGACY ✯ ✯

James Monroe was the last of the Founding Fathers to hold the nation's highest seat of power. Riding his predecessor's coattails, Monroe was elected to the presidency by a landslide and, in fact, ran for reelection unopposed in his second term.

Representing the only viable party at the time, Monroe led the nation in the Era of Good Feelings and spent more time leading the nation than in political infighting. As such, Monroe's accomplishments were aggressive and decidedly impactful on the nation's growth. During his presidency, Monroe was captivated by the idea of western expansion all the way to the Pacific Ocean. Through a series of negotiations and threats, America secured Spain's consent to relinquish many of its North American holdings in favor of the United States. Under Monroe, commerce increased through a commerce treaty with Britain. A staunch nurturer of nationalism, Monroe formulated a policy that came to be known as the Monroe Doctrine, an assertion that none of the European powers were to continue their colonization efforts in the Western Hemisphere.

For these blessings we owe to Almighty God, from which we derive them, and with profound reverence, our most grateful and unceasing acknowledgments.
—Eighth Annual Address, December 7, 1824

Born in Virginia and an ally of Jefferson, Monroe heralded the end of infancy for the nation. Moving from a time when travel was a slow proposition and economic potentials were limited to a specific geographic region to a new era of factories and steamboats, Monroe's presidency spanned an aggressive period of commercial and industrial development. His success was hampered, though, by a dispute that would plague later presidencies and, ultimately, bring the nation to the brink of war several times. That plague was the continuing struggle between the slave states of the South and the free states of the North. Monroe's compromise between these two parties was admitting Maine as a free state, Missouri as a slave state, and abolishing slavery in any state north or west of Missouri. This bill was called the Missouri Compromise.

His previous exploits included service in the military, where he served with no small distinction. Later, as a senator and minister to France, he helped negotiate the Louisiana Purchase. In the 1820 election, Monroe received every electoral vote save one. That one vote held out because a New Hampshire delegate wanted George Washington to be the only unanimously elected president.

After Monroe's second term, he followed Washington's lead of stepping down without a third term and went home

to Virginia before heading to New York, where he died on
July 4, 1831.

✯ ✯ His Faith ✯ ✯

As had his predecessors before him, Monroe stood in
front of the White House on a frosty morning and remembered to give honor to the One who controlled his nation's
destiny:

> I enter on the trust to which I have been called by
> the suffrage of my fellow-citizens with my fervent
> prayers to the Almighty that He will be graciously
> pleased to continue to us that protect which He has
> already so conspicuously displayed in our favor.
> —First Inaugural Address,
> March 4, 1817

May our faith in God bring honor to the One who guides
our nation into the future.

✯ ✯ Faith in Action ✯ ✯

*For every blessing You have poured out, I thank You.
Let me fulfill the purpose You have called me to and
rely on Your protection each day. I continue to trust
in Your favor and guidance, and I pray that You
will use me for Your will, God. Guide our nation
and our president, and let him look to You for each
decision. Let our leader rely on Your protection and
seek Your will. Amen.*

JOHN QUINCY ADAMS

Born: July 11, 1767,
in Braintree, Massachusetts

★ ★ ★ ★

PRESIDENT: 1825–1829

A shaded grove of trees tempers the heat of the sun. Standing beside the trees is a group of citizens celebrating the right to call themselves Americans that this Independence Day offers. Opining on the tenets of the Revolution, John Quincy Adams interjects the following:

> The highest glory of the American Revolution was this: it connected in one indissoluble bond the principles of civil government with the principles of Christianity.
>
> —JULY 4, 1821

★ ★ HIS LIFE ★ ★

*J*ohn Quincy Adams was the son of the nation's second president, John Adams. It was the first such time that any relatives, let alone father and son, had held the highest office of the land.

Growing up in the shadow of his father, John Adams, the second president of the United States, had some effect on John Quincy's success. His father took Adams to Europe when he was still in his impressionable years, and it was there that he became immersed in the languages and the culture. Enrolling in European schools and integrating with the local diplomatic circles, Adams found himself traveling throughout Europe, particularly Germany and Russia, as an interpreter. When he returned to the States to attend Harvard and begin the practice of law, Adams already had a great command of languages and foreign affairs that would serve him well as president. It is said that his mother, Abigail, groomed young John Quincy Adams to become president and reminded him that some day the responsibility for the States would rest upon his shoulders.

✶ ✶ HIS LEGACY ✶ ✶

*A*dams's election signified an almost changing of the guard to a new generation of leadership. These leaders were the sons of the revolutionaries. While they had not participated on the forefront of the creation of the new country, they had seen their parents craft a nation, and they were eager to take over the helm. As the son of the first father-son presidential pair, John Quincy Adams was a leader whose ideas needed a strong popular following that Adams seemed unable to garner. Working under poorly executed strategies, his policies languished in part because he could not play the "game" of politics. Too diplomatic a man to attack his enemies, he allowed them to openly criticize him. Those critics eventually rallied behind Andrew Jackson, who would go on to defeat Adams in the next election.

The first and almost the only Book deserving of universal attention is the Bible.

Before his election in 1824, Adams served in Congress in both the Senate and House; he also represented American interests abroad in Europe. One notable crusade of Adams's early years was an eight-year battle against a rule that had been enacted by southern congressmen to stifle any attempt at even discussing bills aimed at ending slavery. He was eventually successful, and the rule was repealed. Two interesting firsts for this president were that he was the first to be photographed and the first to be interviewed by a female reporter.

✶ ✶ HIS FAITH ✶ ✶

Adams's faith was often a source of inspiration to his own son, to whom he wrote a series of letters about the Bible that were later published by the *New York Tribune*. He further encouraged him by declaring that it was his common practice to read several chapters of the Bible each morning to help him prepare for his day. John Quincy Adams grew up with a strong Christian heritage that he continued in both his personal and political life.

Although he had a strong pedigree, Adams's initial election was marred by controversy. No candidate in the 1824 election had received a majority of the vote and, consequently, the election went to the lower house of Congress, who elected Adams. In 1828, after such a fiasco and lackluster presidency, Adams was content to retire to his family farm.

If John Quincy Adams were asked about the separation of church and state or the removal of God from government, there is little doubt that he would see no purpose in such a question. When he stood outside in front of his assembled fellow Americans to take the oath of office one spring morning, he believed that he was standing before more than just man. His words were not meant for human ears alone, but those words crossed the threshold into the very presence of heaven.

> I appear, my fellow-citizens, in your presence and in that of heaven to by myself by the solemnities of religious obligation to the faithful performance of the duties allotted to me... With fervent supplications for His favor, to His overruling providence I commit with humble but fearless confidence my own fate and the future destinies of my country.
> —INAUGURAL ADDRESS, MARCH 4, 1825

Surprisingly though, he was elected in 1830 by his home district to the House of Representatives, where he served for more than a decade as an influential and successful statesman until he collapsed on that very floor. He was the first president to hold public office after the presidency.

✶ ✶ FAITH IN ACTION ✶ ✶

Lord, let us never believe that for a moment we are out of Your sight. We stand before You in all things. Forgive us for living our lives believing that our actions are hidden from You. It is with fearless confidence that I hand over the control of my life, my family, and my nation to You. Amen.

ANDREW JACKSON

*Born: March 15, 1767,
in Waxhaw, South Carolina*

★ ★ ★ ★

PRESIDENT: 1829–1837

When Andrew Jackson assumed the presidency, many thought they had elected a "man of the people" and a "man's man." Famous for his military prowess, his public manner, and his tendency to duel whenever provoked by comments about his wife, Jackson created an era called Jacksonian Democracy, which the public saw as being an advocate for the majority against powerful corrupt influences plaguing the country. His rise from frontiersman to soldier to president reaffirmed the notion that good things can come to all and bolstered the faith of the American people.

★ ★ HIS LIFE ★ ★

Growing up in the countryside of the Carolinas, Jackson had a limited education, but that did not stop him from pursuing it. He later became a lawyer. In 1791, he married Rachel Donelson, who had been previously married. Rachel's first husband, however, never obtained permission to divorce. After the divorce was granted, the Jacksons remarried in 1794. Although they never had children of their own, they did open their home to many children.

Jackson was the first president to have ever been a prisoner of war and the first to ever use the railroad. He lived for almost forty years with a bullet lodged near his heart after being wounded in a duel with Charles Dickinson, who had insulted his wife and whom Jackson ultimately killed.

The Bible is the Rock on which this Republic rests.

☆ ☆ HIS LEGACY ☆ ☆

In early spring, hundreds gathered to get their first look at their new president. His first words would tell the nation if it had chosen wisely. These words mark the end of Jackson's first speech as president:

> And a firm reliance on the goodness of that Power whose providence mercifully protected our national infancy, and has since upheld our liberties in various vicissitudes, encourages me to offer up my ardent supplications that He will continue to make our beloved country the object to His divine care and gracious benediction.
>
> —First Inaugural Address,
> March 4, 1829

Andrew Jackson's ascent to the presidency was an unusual one. After decrying the previous election in which he felt that a vast conspiracy had caused him to lose, he focused on campaigning on his war record and popular support.

Jackson, a national hero with strong southern support, was elected in a manner that closely resembled the modern-day election strategies of both parties. The first president since Washington to have served in the organized American military, Jackson had very little formal education but managed to lead the nation to a couple of milestones. Under his presidency the national debt was fully paid and a new political party (the Whigs) emerged. President Jackson's use of the powers of the office and his methods have led many historians to call Jackson the first of the modern-day presidents.

Jackson was an able leader. As a general during the battle of New Orleans, he was the only president to see action in the Revolution and the War of 1812. Prior to the war, Jackson was a Supreme Court justice in the state of Tennessee and a member of both the House and Senate. After the war, he became governor of Florida and regained a seat in the Senate. His style was very straightforward, and he carried it into the presidency. Jackson believed that he was the direct representative of the common man and that political office should belong to the most deserving rather than just the politically popular. This view brought him great popular support and an easy reelection in 1832, but often Jackson would lock horns with Congress over his ideals. In 1835 though, the United States finally repaid its debts in full for the first time in history. As in war, Jackson fought many grueling battles over political appointments and the economic policies of the country, and, more often than not, he won.

✯ ✯ HIS FAITH ✯ ✯

After having been elected to a second term, Jackson again faces a crowd one early spring in Washington. Again he makes clear his reliance on God by offering this request for his nation:

Finally, it is my most fervent prayer to that Almighty Being before whom I now stand, and who has kept us in His hands from the infancy of our Republic to the present day, that He will so overrule all my intentions and actions and inspire the hearts of my fellow-citizens that we may be preserved from dangers of all kinds and continue forever a united and happy people.

—SECOND INAUGURAL ADDRESS,
MARCH 4, 1833

Following his two terms in office, Jackson did not seek reelection for a third term but instead retired. He lived to be seventy-eight and died in Nashville, Tennessee.

✳ ✳ FAITH IN ACTION ✳ ✳

Lord, I pray that You will rule in me. In my life and action let me inspire the hearts of those around me for You. I pray for this nation and that You forever keep us a united people who look toward Your Word for guidance. Let me firmly rely on Your power each day. Amen.

MARTIN VAN BUREN

Born: December 5, 1782,
in Columbia, New York

★ ★ ★ ★

PRESIDENT: 1837–1841

*W*ithout a doubt, Martin Van Buren's close alliance with his predecessor, Andrew Jackson, was significantly important to his career. Jackson fought hard with those in his administration who blocked Van Buren's advancement. Jackson was ultimately successful in getting his disciple into a position to take over the reins.

★ ★ HIS LIFE ★ ★

*R*aised and educated in Kinderhook, New York, Martin Van Buren graduated from the Kinderhook Academy. His upbringing was a simple one. The son of a farmer, Martin Van Buren was the first president to be born in the formalized United States of America. His lasting contribution was the introduction of the term *OK*. Originally used during his election campaign to stand for his nickname "Old Kinderhook," it has now come to have the meaning we know today as "all right."

Growing up in a close-knit Dutch community, Van Buren married his cousin, Hannah Hoes. Very little is known about her because Van Buren, being the gentleman that he was, excluded her name from his autobiography. Church records, however, reveal some details of her life, as church affiliation was important to the Van Burens. Both Martin and Hannah were deeply committed to their faith. At the time of Hannah's death, the *Albany Argus* called her "an ornament of the Christian faith." Martin Van Buren also left a legacy of faith in his life. An adherent of the Dutch Reformed Church, Martin Van Buren, as Jackson said, was a "true man without guile."

But notwithstanding these adverse circumstances, that general prosperity which has been heretofore so bountifully bestowed upon us by the Author of All Good still continues to call for our warmest gratitude.
—*Third Annual Message, December 2, 1839*

★ ★ HIS LEGACY ★ ★

Unfortunately, though, everything during the term of Martin Van Buren was not "all right." With banks and businesses failing, America headed into the worst depression on record. Martin Van Buren's presidential term was spoiled by these troubling financial issues. Although he struggled valiantly to stem the economic tide, the country entered a period of extreme financial hardship that both he and his detractors had no idea how to counteract. His goal then became to maintain the financial solvency of the Republic at all costs. One interesting financial tidbit is that Van Buren did not take a salary each year, but rather he chose to receive a lump sum of $100,000 at the end of his term.

Trained as a lawyer, he held many state posts in New York and later several positions within Jackson's administration. His early career was marked by a striking loyalty to Andrew Jackson, and it served both of them well. When Van Buren lost reelection to the Whig party in 1840, his loss symbolized the Whigs' first national political victory. Ironically, one tactic used by the Whigs was to portray Van Buren as an aristocrat with a high society upbringing while his opponent was a man of the people. In truth, those two backgrounds were reversed in the persons of Van Buren and Harrison. Ultimately, though, the Whigs were successful and won the office. Although he ran for reelection three times, Van Buren could not recapture national favor. He died in Kinderhook, New York.

☆ ☆ HIS FAITH ☆ ☆

Another new president walks up in front of well-wishers and fellow public servants. The time has come to tell the nation of the plans of the new leader. These first words will set the tone for the next four years. With care, Van Buren uses them to turn his audience's attention to the sky above:

> Beyond that I only look to the gracious protection
> of the Divine Being whose strengthening support
> I humbly solicit, and whom I fervently pray to look
> down upon us all. May it be among the dispensa-
> tions of His providence to bless our beloved coun-
> try with honors and with length of days. May her
> ways be ways of pleasantness and all her paths be
> peace!
> —INAUGURAL ADDRESS, MARCH 4, 1837

Knowing he has not been reelected, Van Buren uses one of his last chances to capture the nation's attention by imparting these words at the close of his last national address:

> Our devout gratitude is due to the Supreme Being for having graciously continued to our beloved country through the vicissitudes of another year the invaluable blessings of health, plenty, and peace.
>
> —FOURTH ANNUAL MESSAGE,
> DECEMBER 5, 1840

May our faith never waver in the face of poverty.

✴ ✴ FAITH IN ACTION ✴ ✴

In times of plenty and in times of want, I look to You, God. Even in my most difficult times, I know that You are there guiding me. Help me to walk in Your ways each day regardless of the world around me, and grant me Your gracious protection and support. Amen.

WILLIAM HENRY HARRISON

Born: February 9, 1773, in Charles City County, Virginia

★ ★ ★ ★

PRESIDENT: 1841

*I*t seems ironic that one of the shortest-lived presidencies can yield one of the strongest examples of presidential faith and reliance on God. Harrison may have lacked brevity in his speech, but certainly this eloquent statement shows his heart:

> I deem the present occasion sufficiently impor-
> tant and solemn to justify me in expressing to
> my fellow-citizens a profound reverence for the
> Christian religion and a thorough conviction that
> sound morals, religious liberty, and a just sense of
> religious responsibility are essentially connected
> with all true and lasting happiness...
>
> —INAUGURAL ADDRESS,
> MARCH 4, 1841

Although Harrison represented a major victory for his newly formed party, it was short lived. Many know Harrison only as the shortest-serving president ever. In truth, however, Harrison's accomplishments go well beyond his short term in office.

As America moved from an agrarian society into the Industrial Age, citizens of the new nation began having smaller families. Less farming meant less work, which quickly translated into fewer children needed to work the farm. Harrison was one of the last presidents to have an extremely large family with over ten children, and his family had an almost equal number of boys and girls.

Famous as "Old Tip" for the battle of Tippecanoe, Harrison received many votes based on his military service and subsequent popularity. His military service was his main claim to fame. He held the usual posts in Congress and a few positions on the frontier. Immediately before his election, Harrison was actually a county court clerk. Yet the public remembered their hero, and Harrison was brought to power with the slogan "Tippecanoe and Tyler too" that advertised the Whigs party ticket. Amusingly, both President Harrison and Vice President John Tyler were born in the same county, the only successful presidential pair with that distinction.

...to that good Being who has blessed us by the gifts of civil and religious freedom, who watched over and prospered the labors of our fathers and has hither to preserved to us institutions far exceeding in excellence those of any other people, let us unite in fervently commending every interest of our beloved country in all future time.

—Inaugural Address, March 4, 1841

Harrison had begun medical school but switched tracks to take a commission in the First Infantry of the Regular Army and headed off to serve on the northwestern frontier. He rose in the ranks from ensign to general with an almost two-decade long break partly spent as governor of the Indiana Territory.

✶ ✶ HIS LEGACY ✶ ✶

Once in office, Harrison really did not have much time to show the caliber of his presidency. Medicine, not being quite as advanced as it is today, was often unable to cure diseases that we see today as merely inconvenient. Many times common illness could be fatal, such as the one that sealed this president's fate. Various sources differ, however, as to how Harrison contracted pneumonia. Some say it was because of his 105-minute-long inaugural speech in the cold; others say it was because he went to the market for groceries without a hat; and yet, others blame it on his riding in a open-topped carriage shortly after the election. All these stories have one common thread: Harrison, in the cold, without proper clothing. Adding to the nation's problems were an unknown vice president and a process for presidential succession that had never been tried before. The result was a dead president, a confused government, and two very frustrated political parties.

✶ ✶ HIS FAITH ✶ ✶

History shows that Harrison was not overly active in the church until he reached the presidency. Some have speculated that he was so haggard after the election with job seekers and political opponents constantly confronting him that he turned to his religion for strength. One of the pastors at Harrison's funeral recorded that he had been actively participating in church since taking office and was scheduled to have a detailed discussion with the pastor the next Sunday regarding his faith.

> At half past 11 o'clock, the Rev. Mr. Hawley, Rector of St. John's Church, arose, and observed that he would mention an incident connected with the Bible which lay on the table before him (covered with black silk velvet). "This Bible," said he, "was purchased by the President on the fifth of March. He has since been in the habit of daily reading it. He was accustomed not only to attend church, but to join audibly in the services, and to kneel humbly before his maker."

Let us not make our dependency on God a crutch upon which we lean during difficult times only, but let us acknowledge our dependence upon Him even when things appear to be going well. We should pray, in faith, at all times, in all types of circumstances, with the knowledge that He is the One who directs our steps.

✶ ✶ FAITH IN ACTION ✶ ✶

God, I come to You with a profound reverence for who You are and what You have done in my life. Each day You have watched over my family and me and guided the labors of our hands. Your every blessing exceeds my expectations, Lord, and I thank You. Let me rely on You every day for the rest of my life. Amen.

JOHN TYLER

Born: March 29, 1790,
in Greenway, Virginia

★ ★ ★ ★

PRESIDENT: 1841–1845

$\mathscr{J}$ohn Tyler was thrust into the spotlight by unexpected circumstances. His successful assumption of the reins of power showed the forethought of the Founding Fathers and the widespread commitment to democracy that is endemic in America. Rather than derail the succession process, both political parties supported Tyler's right to become president. If there ever was time for questioning that process, Tyler provided the perfect test case. A relative unknown to the American public and even to many of the political elite, Tyler initially paired with Harrison more out of necessity rather than desire.

★ ★ HIS LIFE ★ ★

$\mathscr{H}$umorously called "His Accidency" by many, Tyler was the first president to become so by way of his predecessor's demise. He was still unknown. He had never run for the office of president and had been put on the "Old Tip" ticket to balance it against the opposing party. Sadly, both political parties quickly abandoned the new president because they were eager to take sides in the upcoming election that offered the possibility to reelect Martin Van Buren.

✻ ✻ HIS LEGACY ✻ ✻

*D*espite many difficulties, Tyler still tried hard to make his presidency a success. He was plagued by a hostile cabinet that resigned en mass, and his first wife died while he was in office. His presidency saw the beginning of trade with China and an attempt to annex the territory of Texas that would eventually lead to war with Mexico. Initially Tyler failed to get approval to annex Texas, but following the next election, Congress agreed to the annexation. On Tyler's last day in office, he invited Texas to join the United States.

The world has witnessed its rapid growth in wealth and population, and under the guide and direction of the superintending Providence the developments of the past may be regarded but as the shadowing forth of the mighty future.
—Fourth Annual Message, December 3, 1844

In earlier years, Tyler had been quite active in the politics of his home state. For more than two decades, he held various positions within Virginia's government, eventually becoming the governor, until he quickly made his way to the Senate. One might be inclined to think that with fifteen children at home, all but one of whom made it through infancy, Tyler would be too busy to do anything other than parent.

Since his party declined to nominate him for the election, Tyler was forced out of office without ever having a chance to run on his own merit. John Tyler would later become quite significant when the first southern states seceded in 1861 because he attempted to reach a compromise between North and South. When those efforts failed, he worked to create the Confederacy, where he would later hold office until he died the next year.

✦ ✦ HIS FAITH ✦ ✦

Congressmen wait on the president to deliver his words to sum up the year. It is 1843, and the December snow rages outside the building. Standing to the front of this group is the president, who solemnly remarks:

> If any people ever had cause to render up thanks to the Supreme Being for parental care and protection extended to them in all the trials and difficulties to which they have been from time to time exposed, we certainly are that people.
> —THIRD ANNUAL MESSAGE, DECEMBER 1843

As before, having not been elected to another term, Tyler has one last opportunity to impart words of wisdom for the country and its people. On a cold winter day, Tyler concludes his last national address with these words:

> We have continued cause for expressing our gratitude to the Supreme Ruler of the Universe for the benefits and blessings which our country, under His kind providence, has enjoyed during the past year.
> — FOURTH ANNUAL MESSAGE,
> DECEMBER 3, 1844

✳ ✳ FAITH IN ACTION ✳ ✳

Lord God, as I look back over what You have done in my past, let me see it as but a foreshadowing of what You have in my future. Thank You for guiding my life, my family, and my nation. Let me cede each day to Your direction and trust in Your providence to guide me. Amen.

JAMES KNOX POLK

Born: November 2, 1795, in Mecklenburg County, North Carolina

✫ ✫ ✫ ✫

PRESIDENT: 1845–1849

*I*f in the twenty-first century, a ruler stood up and said that without God a nation may be damaged by its leaders, the press would probably laugh, the citizens would despair, and the world would be agape. Yet that is precisely what Polk did, and the people respected and agreed with it. On this Tuesday, dozens stood in the pouring rain to hear Polk's speech.

> In assuming responsibilities so vast I fervently invoke the aid of that Almighty Ruler of the Universe in whose hands are the destinies of nations and of men to guard this Heaven-favored land against the mischiefs, which without His guidance might arise from an unwise public policy. With a firm reliance upon the wisdom of Omnipotence to sustain and direct me in the path of duty which I am appointed to pursue.
> —INAUGURAL ADDRESS, MARCH 4, 1845

✶ ✶ HIS LIFE ✶ ✶

*P*olk, as did most American settlers of the day, believed in "Manifest Destiny." They believed it was their God-given mission in life to expand the borders of the young nation and extend democratic ideals to all.

Much modernization did occur during Polk's one term. Gaslights began to replace candles and other obsolete sources of illumination in the White House. News of Polk's nomination was carried over the newly invented telegraph and represents one of the first widely distributed news flashes. Polk married a young woman named Sarah Childress on New Year's Day in 1824. Sadly, they had no children together. She would outlive her husband by more than four decades.

✶ ✶ HIS LEGACY ✶ ✶

*T*he election of James Polk marked several significant occurrences. He was the last of his party to hold the office and the last strong leader for the next several years. Most importantly, his election and the transfer of power from Tyler solidified the policies for presidential succession.

...that Divine Being who has watched over and protected our beloved country from its infancy to the present hour to continue His gracious benedictions upon us, that we may continue to be a prosperous and happy people.

—Inaugural Address, March 4, 1845

Elected by a narrow margin, James Polk had only a slim lead in the popular vote but captured a good deal more electoral votes than his opponent, Henry Clay, in part because of a third unofficial candidate that siphoned potentially key votes. Polk now had the chance to craft the growing nation. Under the prevailing ideals of "Manifest Destiny," Polk sought to bring the borders of the Union from sea to sea and oust the British and Mexican claims that held some of these territories. It was this desire that would in part lead to war with Mexico during his term. The result was inclusion of most of the modern-day western states. This expansion reopened the rift previously sealed by legislation such as the Missouri Compromise. Although the agreement was for states north and west of Missouri to be free, few southern states had considered the possibility of just how many potential states lay to the west. Thus Polk was hedged in by a populace clamoring for expansion and southern congressmen who saw expansion as a threat to slavery. The tides of discontent between North and South were starting to wash in stronger than ever before.

Polk's policies and bloody war led to general dissatisfaction in his political party. Whether owing either to that dissatisfaction or to his failing health, he was not even nominated for reelection. However, when his term ended, it had achieved one momentous goal: by 1849, the United States had stretched from the Atlantic to the Pacific. James Polk died in 1849 just a few months after leaving office.

✵ ✵ HIS FAITH ✵ ✵

Only the second Presbyterian to hold office, James Polk and his wife served the first annual Thanksgiving dinner in the

White House. Polk's wife, Sarah, was a devout Presbyterian and put her convictions into action by quickly banning dancing, card playing, and alcohol in the White House. A week before James Polk died, he was baptized as a Methodist.

✮ ✮ FAITH IN ACTION ✮ ✮

Jesus, with firm reliance on Your power and the knowledge that You alone hold supreme authority, I ask You to direct the destiny of my life. Put me on the path I am appointed to pursue, and keep me from straying. Protect us against the unwise who would seek to destroy our nation or my life. Your leading and protection are what allow us to continue to be a prosperous and happy people. Amen.

ZACHARY TAYLOR

Born: November 24, 1784,
in Orange County, Virginia

★ ★ ★ ★

PRESIDENT: 1849–1850

Taylor, probably more than any president yet, faced the fear that the Union his forefathers had worked so hard to create might be divided. Instead of trying to blame others or shaking his fist, he humbly relied on God's guidance:

> During the past year we have been blessed by a kind Providence with an abundance of the fruits of the earth, and although the destroying angel for a time visited extensive portions of our territory with the ravages of a dreadful pestilence, yet the Almighty has at length deigned to stay his hand and to restore the inestimable blessing of general health to a people who have acknowledged His power, deprecated His wrath, and implored His merciful protection.
> —ANNUAL MESSAGE, DECEMBER 4, 1849

★ ★ HIS LIFE ★ ★

At this time in American history, slavery was a hot issue with the country evenly divided. What was once an issue of mere antagonism had become a central theme as southerners began to feel that their very way of life was threatened. Fanning the flames further was the possibility that two new large states may be coming into statehood, New Mexico and California, and their status on slavery was undetermined. Taylor, in an attempt to find a compromise on the issue, sent a proposal to Congress to allow two huge conglomerate states of the west into the Union. In addition, the plan called for direct statehood, thus bypassing the traditional "territory" phase. Instead of acting as a compromise, Taylor's request set the stage for the possibility of his greatest fear, civil war. When Taylor met with the congressional leaders, northern politicians were upset that Taylor had, in their view, usurped their power. Then the southern leadership began to threaten secession. What finally broke the deadlock was General, not President, Taylor who informed the southern states that if they seceded, he would personally lead the army against the South and hang anyone supporting the rebellion. Needless to say, his past experience and present conviction made a convincing case, and war was averted.

✦ ✦ HIS LEGACY ✦ ✦

Another brief term in office, Zachary Taylor went from being a general at war with Mexico to the president of the United States in rapid sequence.

A career soldier, Taylor was nominated for president, which came as a complete surprise to many. Since he refused to pay the postage on the notice of nomination sent to him, the nomination came as an especially large surprise for him. Taylor was a complete mystery to the American public and to Washington insiders as well. As a general, he had won fame by leading the army against General Santa Anna in the Mexican War of the last administration when he beat a force that outnumbered his by more than four to one.

In conclusion I congratulate you, my fellow-citizens, upon the high state of prosperity to which the goodness of Divine Providence has conducted our common country. Let us invoke a continuance of the same protecting care which has led us from small beginnings to the eminence we this day occupy...
—Inaugural Address, March 5, 1849

Amazingly for a president, Taylor had never before held public office. In fact, he was the first president who had not done so. He had no formal education. Although he owned a cotton farm, he ironically did not defend slavery or many other southern positions. He avoided politics by never speaking out publicly on any issue and, in fact, never voted (not even for himself). Taylor's appeal lay solely in his war record. Thus, the hope was that a war hero who owned slaves but did not defend slavery would make an attractive national candidate.

Taylor's success was very short lived. After participating in Independence Day ceremonies, he reportedly consumed tainted cherries and milk, which made him sick, and he died. What was to have been a settled issue dropped directly into the lap of vice president turned president Millard Fillmore. Eleven years after Zachary Taylor's death, his son, Richard Taylor, would fight in the war his father tried so hard to avoid as a general for the Confederacy.

✶ ✶ His Faith ✶ ✶

Although ill at ease taking a stand on political issues, Taylor made it very clear in whom he trusted. How incredible that a president who had not asserted his beliefs on policy and who sought compromise would be so unequivocal in his declaration of thanks and reliance on God:

> It is a proper theme of thanksgiving to Him who rules the destinies of nations that we have been able to maintain amidst all these contests an independent and neutral position toward all belligerent powers.
>
> —Annual Message, December 4, 1849

✶ ✶ Faith in Action ✶ ✶

Although from time to time life may be hard, Father, You have always provided and restored me. In a time of national concern, we look to You for Your hand of blessing and implore Your merciful protection on us and those around us. Let us live in harmony in the midst of conflict and look to You for our relief. Amen.

MILLARD FILLMORE

Born: January 7, 1800,
in Cayuga County, New York

★ ★ ★ ★

PRESIDENT: 1850–1853

Millard Fillmore was another president who ascended to the office by way of an unfortunate death. Succeeding Zachary Taylor, who had struggled to hold the Union together in the midst of deepening polarization between North and South, Fillmore was at a point of decision. There existed in Congress two options to address the looming crisis. One was to allow the nation to split over the issues of slavery and new statehood for western territories. The other option, which Fillmore took, was to back a bill in Congress initially called the Omnibus Bill. That bill was a grouping of several "compromise" legislations that would address the northern concerns about continued slavery and, at the same time, protect the slave-driven economies of the South. This bill would become known as the Compromise of 1850. Although the combined bill itself failed, each component was passed by Congress, and for a short time longer, a showdown involving the North, South, and the government had been averted.

As a young man, Fillmore's early years were spent not in the cities of the East but on the frontier lands in a log cabin. Attending school in the now quintessential one-room school of the frontier, Fillmore received an education and eventually married his teacher, Abigail Powers. After a stint in law and state government, Fillmore went from state comptroller of New York to the vice presidency. Many point to his story as a fine example of living the American Dream where one can go from obscurity to fame through hard work and diligence. More humble than most, Fillmore refused an honorary degree from Oxford because he believed he had not achieved anything of merit. This was the same man who was the first to install a library in the White House.

The man who can look upon a crisis without being willing to offer himself upon the altar of his country is not for public trust.

—Source Unknown

✳ ✳ His Legacy ✳ ✳

Although he lent his support to the Compromise of 1850, few credited that success to Fillmore who was instead left to finish out the remainder of his predecessor's term. When it came time to elect the next president, Fillmore was not even a contender. Later, however, Fillmore would represent the Know-Nothing and American Party in the next election. A success story in overall terms, Fillmore could never fully untangle himself from the secessionist battles raging around him. The remainder of his post-government career was spent as the chancellor for the University of Buffalo.

★ ★ HIS FAITH ★ ★

In the wake of another national tragedy, another president stands before the leaders of a grieving nation. What words of comfort can he bring? The members of Congress each see their nation's fate reflected in the man before them. His predecessor has avoided civil war. Where can he find the strength to lead?

> I rely upon Him who holds in His hands the destinies of nations to endow me with the requisite strength for the task and to avert from our country the evils apprehended from the heavy calamity, which has befallen us.
> —ADDRESS TO CONGRESS AFTER
> TAKING THE OATH OF OFFICE, JULY 9, 1850

We may face various trials and opposition during our lifetime, but we can rely upon God who is the Source of our strength in times of trouble (Ps. 37:39).

✷ ✷ FAITH IN ACTION ✷ ✷

Father, once again our nation is divided along the lines of morality. We have become desensitized to what is right and good. We ask You, Lord, to forgive us and have mercy upon us as a nation. Place godly men and women in positions of authority in our country. When evil threatens our lives, give us Your strength, wisdom, and guidance. In Jesus' name, amen.

FRANKLIN PIERCE

Born: November 23, 1804, in
Hillsboro, New Hampshire

✯ ✯ ✯ ✯

PRESIDENT: 1853–1857

*G*reeting the nation for the first time, Pierce has more questions swirling in his head than answers. His faith shows him where and to whom to look for answers. And then the thought strikes him. You can almost hear the question resound in Franklin Pierce's mind: *What would happen if God took a break?* Thankfully, we never have to worry about God taking a break.

Pierce correctly traced every step of American independence to the grace and wisdom with which the Lord blessed the forefathers. Moreover, Pierce asserted that the continued blessing of our heavenly Father is the greatest of all hopes for the nation:

> The energy with which that great conflict was opened and, under the guidance of a manifest and beneficent Providence, the uncomplaining endurance with which it was prosecuted to its consummation were only surpassed by the wisdom and patriotic spirit of concession which characterized all the counsels of the early fathers.
>
> —INAUGURAL ADDRESS, MARCH 4, 1853

✲ ✲ His Life ✲ ✲

After an election where the parties tried so hard not to upset the delicate compromise reached under the previous administration, the campaigns of 1852 were quite unspectacular. Nonetheless, Franklin Pierce defeated his Whig opponent, who was formerly his commanding general in the Mexican War, by a significant margin. Although he was a lesser-known leader from New Hampshire, it would fall to Pierce to navigate the seemingly calmed waters between northern industrialization and southern slavery.

Added to these national concerns was a much deeper and private disaster for the Pierce family: their eleven-year-old son, Benjamin, was killed in a railroad accident shortly after the election. It was the third child the Pierces had lost. The accident occurred when the railcar that the Pierces were riding derailed and fell into an embankment. The only person injured was their son.

✲ ✲ His Legacy ✲ ✲

Pierce was a striking mix of traits and experiences. He publicly gave a three-thousand-word address from memory, yet, by the second year of college, he had the lowest grades of his class. He later catapulted his academic performance to finish the rest of his studies as third in his class. Unrivaled still today, Pierce is the only president to keep all of his cabinet members for the entire term. Such unbelievable highs and lows were the hallmark of Pierce's life and career.

Although he attempted to stay on a middle road between the factions, Pierce was decried by one or both sides for everything he did as president. One or both parties looked at every decision, no matter how neutral or how beneficial to the nation, as a partisan act. Any attempt at expansion was seen as an attempt to bring in either more slave or free states. Such tensions stymied growth and weakened the compromise that kept the peace. When hostilities broke out in Kansas between proslavery and abolitionist factions, the compromise was at the end of its life. Further exacerbated by a repeal of the Missouri Compromise, the nation was firmly headed down the path to civil war. Although he could claim a resolution in Kansas, Pierce had so alienated his party by trying to walk a tightrope that they declined to renominate him. After his term, he lived for more than a decade in retirement, spending time in part by enjoying his love for fishing.

I can express no better hope for my country than that the kind Providence which smiled upon our fathers may enable their children to preserve the blessings they have inherited.

—*Inaugural Address, March 4, 1853*

✯ ✯ HIS FAITH ✯ ✯

All of the turmoil that marked Pierce's personal and public life, however, did not dissuade him from his faith. Sources record that because of his religious convictions about swearing an oath, he instead chose to "affirm" the oath of office. He was also the first president to prominently display his faith by erecting, in the winter, the first White House Christmas tree. Although plagued by misfortune, Pierce never forgot the source of his strength through both trouble and victory.

In a time when "terror" was not the watchword of the day, Pierce, nevertheless, understood that the day-to-day safety of the nation was guaranteed only by its dependence on God. Weapons and armies might be a measure of human strength, but security is provided by something much more potent.

> It must be felt that there is no national security but in the nation's humble acknowledged dependence upon God and His overruling providence.
> —INAUGURAL ADDRESS, MARCH 4, 1853

✶ ✶ FAITH IN ACTION ✶ ✶

Thank You, Lord, that in moments of weariness You never falter. Your Spirit guides us each step, and each step we take is directed. Let us not trust in the weapons of man or the strength of world powers to insure our security, but instead rely on You for each day. May we boldly declare "In God we trust." Amen.

JAMES BUCHANAN

*Born: April 23, 1791,
in Cove Gap, Pennsylvania*

★ ★ ★ ★

PRESIDENT: 1857–1861

The nation was crumbling, and Congress, in part, blames the president for his failure to bring healing. James Buchanan stands before an angry Congress, sweat beading on his brow, convinced that although the darkest hour may loom, God has never failed to provide. It is with that conviction that he boldly asserts:

> When we compare the condition of the country at the present day with what it was one year ago at the meeting of Congress, we have much reason for gratitude to that Almighty Providence which has never failed to interpose for our relief at the most critical periods of our history.
> —SECOND ANNUAL ADDRESS TO CONGRESS

★ ★ HIS LIFE ★ ★

Life during these times was quickly unraveling. James Buchanan continued the run of the "one-term presidents." Without a doubt, he came on the scene at a time of national chaos. The political party system was fractured, the nation reeling, and somehow, he was tapped to lead them both.

To get a sense of just how bad things were at this time, one needs to briefly review the current events of that period. For example, a southern senator had brutally beaten, with a cane, a prominent northern senator on the open Senate floor. Another example was the Supreme Court decision in the Dred Scott case that came two days after Buchanan's inauguration. The ruling held that Congress could not ban slavery and that blacks could never become citizens. Among other things, an economic slowdown caused widespread panic. Despite the turbulent times, James Buchanan truly believed he could help keep the peace.

I shall now proceed to take the oath prescribed by the Constitution, whilst humbly invoking the blessing of Divine Providence on this great people.
　　　　　　　　—*Inaugural Address, March 4, 1857*

✴ ✴ HIS LEGACY ✴ ✴

Although he tried his best to bring his skills as a former diplomat to Russia and England to bear, the ideological battle was too far gone. Sadly, the nation fully fractured under Buchanan. He was faced with a House of Representatives that was controlled by the Republicans and a Senate with a Democratic majority. The Senate rejected every bill the House of Representatives passed. Government came to a standstill.

The presidency of James Buchanan heralded a sad time for both the country and those citizens that would be born after. There is no easy way to read about the events that followed, and many today still try to make sense of brother fighting brother. The final significant act of his presidency was for Buchanan to order troops to reinforce Fort Sumter.

Buchanan left office and retired to Pennsylvania where he watched the nation tear itself apart.

✫ ✫ HIS FAITH ✫ ✫

Although faced with some of the worst times in the history of the country, Buchanan held to his belief in God. He recognized that the only Power that could heal a nation rapidly pulling apart at the seams resided in a Being much greater than he.

Knowing that his skill as a diplomat was not enough to bring healing to the deep divisions of the nation, Buchanan stood before America and invoked the power of the greatest Healer and Diplomat:

> In entering upon this great office I must humbly invoke the God of our fathers for wisdom and firmness to execute its high and responsible duties in such a manner as to restore harmony and ancient friendship among the people of the several States and to preserve our free institutions throughout many generations.
> —INAUGURAL ADDRESS, MARCH 4, 1857

Whatever monumental decisions we face, may we never crumble in the face of adversity. May we always exercise our faith in God who is able to sustain us and lift us up.

O Lord, let us never doubt that in moments of trouble, You alone stay constant. Let us look not to others or ourselves for healing but rely on Your Providence, which has guided us this far. We humbly ask You to touch our nation and the issues that divide us. No matter how bleak it may look, You are in control. Amen.

ABRAHAM LINCOLN

Born: February 12, 1809,
in Hodgenville, Kentucky

★ ★ ★ ★

PRESIDENT: 1861–1865

*O*utside of George Washington, Abraham Lincoln might be our most well-known, loved, and cherished president. The country saw some of its hardest times and greatest accomplishments under this man. During his term, the Civil War ripped through the nation, pitting brother against brother. The nation was trapped in an endless hell of war and death, but Lincoln strove for the light at the end of the tunnel.

★ ★ HIS LIFE ★ ★

*I*n addition to the politics and war, Lincoln was also the president of the nation and had to carry out ordinary functions and duties. Lincoln was both the tallest president and the first president to wear a beard, which Lincoln may have worn to hide the facial scars he earned while living on the Midwest frontier.

He married Mary Todd, and they had four boys, only one of whom lived to maturity, Robert. Lacking formal early education, Lincoln worked hard to learn through experience. In his professional life, he was a lawyer and served in his state government. Lincoln was a strong proponent of technology and used the telegraph for battle updates. But since there was not a telegraph machine in the White House, he had to walk to the War Department for updates.

I believe the Bible is the best gift God has ever given to man. All the good from the Savior of the world is communicated to us through this book.

✶ ✶ HIS LEGACY ✶ ✶

To fully understand the climate of the times and the man that would be president, it is important to understand what happened in the election of 1860. Upon the nomination of Stephen Douglas to run for president, the entire southern delegation of the Democratic Party pretty much pulled out of the party. These delegates wanted one of the candidates that was more sensitive to southern concerns but whom the nation at large felt was too extreme on issues such as slavery. Lincoln himself was actually considered a moderate on the issue of slavery and won the election with around 40 percent of the popular vote. What is amazing is that the election of the man who is credited with reuniting the country is also the proximate cause for its initial breakup. This election sealed the secession of the southern states because Lincoln had been elected almost entirely by the support of the northern states. Beginning in December of 1860, the states south of South Carolina began to secede from the Union, eventually forming the Confederacy and electing Jefferson Davis as their president. Although Lincoln was elected to govern the whole nation, by the time of his inauguration, the Union was split. The Confederacy's refusals to allow the resupply of Fort Sumter and the subsequent attack on Fort Sumter began a shooting war between ideas, economics, families, friends, and Americans. In fact, many of Lincoln's own relatives fought against him in the Confederate army.

When it came time for the people to vote again, Lincoln won reelection in 1864 by a landslide. In addition to the votes of normal citizens, some states allowed soldiers to vote in the field, and of those ballots, almost 80 percent of those were for Lincoln. The president rode this public acclaim to push through the Thirteenth Amendment to the Constitution outlawing slavery.

As most school children learn, Lincoln was assassinated by John Wilkes Booth while watching a performance at Ford's Theater. A morbid coincidence is that Lincoln's son, Robert, was present at his assassination in the theater, and Robert was also present when Garfield and McKinley were assassinated.

To this day many historians have debated what more a great man like Lincoln could have done had he lived longer. For one, his death cut short a chance for the South to have peace with honor under the generous terms that Lincoln was prepared to offer. However, what he did accomplish was impressive enough to earn him the endearment of so many generations to come.

☆ ☆ HIS FAITH ☆ ☆

Perhaps Lincoln's best-known personal characteristic was his faith in God.

Few people realize that it is when you are tested that your truest beliefs blaze forth. When left with no other alternative, Lincoln shows his deep-rooted faith by seeking counsel on his knees. Not depending on his armies or his skills, Lincoln humbly reveals his source of strength:

> I have been driven many times to my knees by the overwhelming conviction that I had absolutely no other place to go.

It must have been with a sinking feeling of despair that Lincoln assumed the presidency. It was, in fact, his election that was the final blow to the unity of the nation. To cope with those feelings, what recourse did he have? His words and answer to that question proclaimed the source of his strength in trying times.

In addition to all the domestic pressures, Lincoln still had to interact on the international stage. Standing before powerful world leaders, a gangly president wearing a tall hat asserted this simple truth:

> It is the duty of nations, as well as of men, to own their dependence upon the overruling power of God and to recognize the sublime truth announced in the Holy Scriptures and proven by all history, that those nations only are blessed whose God is the Lord.

✶ ✶ FAITH IN ACTION ✶ ✶

Father, thank You for Your Word and its power. In moments of confusion, let me find wisdom in its pages. Thank You for prayer, Lord Jesus. When I am weak, let me find Your strength on my knees in prayer. I live my life for the purpose of praising You, and I offer thanks for all Your goodness and power. Amen.

ANDREW JOHNSON

Born: December 29, 1808,
in Raleigh, North Carolina

✦ ✦ ✦ ✦

PRESIDENT: 1865–1869

*H*unched over his desk, previous drafts littering the floor around him, Andrew Johnson struggles to find the right words to make Congress see his plan for the nation. Although the war has been won, the rebuilding is far from over, and that task falls on him. But even under that stress, Johnson still makes a point of giving glory to God as the first and last thing his speech seeks to do:

> To express gratitude to God in the name of the people for the preservation of the United States is my first duty in addressing you.... Who of them will not now acknowledge, in the words of Washington, that "every step by which the people of the United States have advanced to the character of an independent nation seems to have been distinguished by some token of providential agency"? Who will not join with me in the prayer that the Invisible Hand which has led us through the clouds that gloomed around our path will so guide us onward to a perfect restoration of fraternal affection.
>
> —FIRST ANNUAL MESSAGE, DECEMBER 4, 1865

✵ ✵ HIS LIFE ✵ ✵

𝒫rior to his life in public office, Johnson was another example of the American Dream. Born into relative obscurity and poverty, Johnson aspired to be a tailor. He later married Eliza McCardle and opened a tailor shop in Greensville, Tennessee. He had a passion for debates. It was that passion for debate that thrusted him into public office. With no real education or status, Johnson went remarkably far. Although he had difficulties as president, Johnson was considered by many to be an honorable and honest lawmaker who was caught in the impossible situation of walking between two warring political camps, very similar to what happened to Fillmore years earlier. Although his failures may have been inevitable, they were still crushing for this president.

An all-wise and merciful Providence has abated the pestilence which visited our shores.
—Second Annual Message, December 3, 1866

After his term in office, Johnson returned to Tennessee where he rejoined the Senate in 1875. He died shortly after being elected.

✵ ✵ HIS LEGACY ✵ ✵

𝒯hrust into leadership at an unbelievable moment, Andrew Johnson was inheriting a nation in grave distress. The South lay in ruin, and the nation's symbol of unity and strength had just been assassinated. Johnson's vice presidency had come as a surprise to many because he and Lincoln were from opposite parties. Lincoln had specifically chosen a pro-war Democrat as his running mate to further attempt to unite the splintered country for the election of 1864. Between the election results and the pushes into Confederate-held territory by Generals Grant, Thomas, and Sherman, the war finally came to a close on April 9, 1865. Five days later an assassin's bullet killed Lincoln and propelled Johnson to the presidency.

As president, Johnson's first and most troubling question was how to go about reconstructing the South. Should he pursue the generous series of pardons and programs aimed at helping the South recover as had been Lincoln's view? Instead Johnson struggled through a maze of overly lenient and then overly harsh decisions and, in the process, stymied the effects of what was known simply as "Reconstruction." These failed policies led to the Republican's gaining a strong majority in Congress during the 1866 election. Things escalated to the point where Johnson was faced with the prospect of impeachment and escaped by only one vote. He would not run for president in the next election.

☆ ☆ HIS FAITH ☆ ☆

So many have talked about God on their deathbed, just moments before seeing Him face to face. What greater tribute than in the final moments of life to be able to proclaim with confidence as Andrew Johnson did shortly before his death:

> I have performed my duty to my God, my country, and my family. I have nothing to fear in approaching death. To me it is the mere shadow of God's protecting wing....Here I will rest in quiet

and peace beyond the reach of calumny's poisoned shaft, the influence of envy and jealous enemies, where treason and traitors or State backsliders and hypocrites in church can have no peace.

—July 31, 1875

✶ ✶ Faith in Action ✶ ✶

Lord, we come before You, first and foremost, to thank You. All that we have comes from You, and Your continued blessings and protection amaze us. We glory in Your Son's sacrifice and trust that on the day we see You face to face, His death will make possible our eternal life. Help us to show that truth to the world around us. Amen.

ULYSSES S. GRANT

Born April 27, 1822,
in Point Pleasant, Ohio

✯ ✯ ✯ ✯

PRESIDENT: 1869–1877

The finest compliment that can be paid to an American is election as leader of the nation. The assembled multitude has come to Washington to see a military leader turned statesman whom the nation can rally behind. Yet, Grant does not take credit for the past successes or responsibility for the future healing. Instead, he rests his calloused hands on the lectern in front and, with his words hanging in the sunshine, points to the Power that will make the Union whole:

> In conclusion, I ask patient forbearance one toward another throughout the land, and a determined effort on the part of every citizen to do his share toward cementing a happy union; and I ask the prayers of the nation to Almighty God in behalf of this consummation.
> —INAUGURAL ADDRESS, MARCH 4, 1869

✩ ✩ HIS LIFE ✩ ✩

U. S. Grant, as he was known to friends at West Point, was originally named Simpson Ulysses Grant, but due to a clerical error his first and middle names were switched. He liked the flair of the "US" so much that he adopted those initials into his signature. Grant was the conquering hero and favorite of the Republican Party. After the debacle of the former president, the Republicans saw in Grant a chance to get the country back on track and were shocked when he was elected by only a small margin of the popular vote. To explain this surprise, many point to Grant's popularity with the recently freed slaves who voted mightily for him and the resulting lack of white southern votes. This caused many Republicans to push for increased black male voting rights. Grant's inauguration parade, however, was that of a national favorite and was the largest ever with over eight full army divisions participating.

No political party can or ought to exist when one of its corner-stones is opposition to freedom of thought and to the right to worship God.
—*Personal Memoirs of Ulysses S. Grant*

✵ ✵ HIS LEGACY ✵ ✵

Remembered by many as the "Hero of Appomattox," Grant was a skilled leader both on and off the battlefield. After a series of successes in the West, Lincoln put Grant in charge of all of the Union troops. When opponents leveled criticisms against Grant's daring and unorthodox tactics, Lincoln replied that Grant would be one of the last he would fire because as he simply observed: "He fights." Lincoln was pointing to a quality that he felt was lacking in General McClellan who commanded the army previously and was so cautious and slow that Lincoln remarked that he would like to "borrow" the army since the general obviously wasn't using it.

U. S. Grant's military career was both spectacular and surprising. Grant graduated from West Point at the bottom of his class and later resigned his commission. During the Civil War, he signed up as a volunteer colonel and was quickly promoted to brigadier general. Grant continued to earn his stars and eventually came to be considered second only to Washington. Those abilities aided him in driving the army to Appomattox Court House where he earned his nickname and accepted the surrender of Confederate General Robert E. Lee. Again surprising many people, Grant showed honor and mercy in his surrender terms and allowed Confederate troops to surrender without fear of treason trials.

As president, Grant used many of the same military skills in governing the nation. Unfortunately, politics and war were often similar in nature but needed to be addressed quite differently, a distinction Grant failed to make. Disillusioned and ill at ease with the political landscape, Grant feared many of his advisors and instead turned to his "Old Guard" friends, leading many to decry what they saw as "cronyism" and scandal. Added to that were the challenges of Reconstruction that were still going on in the South. Yet, Grant won reelection with a good majority of the vote.

✯ ✯ HIS FAITH ✯ ✯

When man's theory came into conflict with God's, U. S. Grant had no confusion as to which should be held superior. For Grant, there was one duty above freedom, and that was the duty to God.

As a member of the Methodist church, U. S. Grant's life and memoirs show his commitment to God. Personally though, Grant was another president with a humble background. Grant felt that everything he did prior to the war was a failure. In business and in school, Grant did not distinguish himself. As the son of a tanner, he worked in a leather shop until he was appointed to lead a group of military misfits whom he promptly whipped into shape. At the end of his life, Grant was involved in a failed business venture when he learned he had throat cancer. In an attempt to settle his debts, he agreed to pen his memoirs. Those memoirs were successful and brought in astounding sales to the tune of almost $500,000. Unfortunately, though, Grant died in 1885 shortly after finishing the last page.

☆ ☆ FAITH IN ACTION ☆ ☆

God, let me be patient with those with whom I come into conflict, and let me show them Your love and mercy. Help me to do my part in making this world a place where You can be praised. Let me never ascribe to an idea or belief that excludes You. Help me to, in all things, praise Your name. Amen.

RUTHERFORD B. HAYES

*Born: October 4, 1822,
in Delaware, Ohio*

✯ ✯ ✯ ✯

PRESIDENT: 1877–1881

*A*fter a hotly contested election, Hayes is finally declared the winner. Speaking to the assembled citizens after having technically been the president for almost forty-eight hours, Hayes retakes the oath on the lawn outside and then discusses his inauguration:

> Looking for the guidance of that Divine Hand by which the destinies of nations and individuals are shaped, I call upon you Senators, Representatives, judges, fellow citizens here and everywhere to unite with me in an earnest effort.
> —INAUGURAL ADDRESS, MARCH 5, 1877

✯ ✯ HIS LIFE ✯ ✯

*H*ayes married Lucy Ware Webb, an unusually well-educated young lady for that day. She was the first First Lady to have graduated from college. Together they had eight children, five of whom survived to adulthood.

Hayes and the First Lady went further in their public displays, holding the first Easter egg hunt on the White

House lawn. Back in those days, however, it was known as an "egg roll."

Many of Rutherford Hayes' policies represented his deep-seated beliefs in equality. He worked hard to promote a better standard of life for the still newly freed slaves. In addition, he made several changes that allowed women more power in government. In addition to those changes of ideas, the White House under Hayes became increasingly more modern and had the first telephone installed by Alexander Graham Bell himself.

✫ ✫ HIS LEGACY ✫ ✫

A very principled man, Hayes would not allow greed to cloud his direction. Winning fame as a general in the Civil War, he was nominated by the Republicans as a representative to Congress. Although flattered by the compliment, he refused the nomination asserting that if he deserted his post as an officer in time of war to take up politics, he deserved to be "scalped." After the war, he served several terms as governor of Ohio and in Congress.

Reconstruction ended in 1877 in just as messy a fashion as it had begun.

In 1876 Hayes, the Republican nominee, lost the popular election, but his opponent was one electoral vote short of winning the election. After some behind-the-scene negotiations, both parties allowed Hayes to assume the presidency under a series of concessions to both sides that would end Reconstruction, try to promote better conditions for blacks in the South, and fund development projects in southern states. This was the backdrop to which Hayes assumed power. There was no real impropriety as much as the election really revealed the failings of the Electoral College. However, the practical results were that the election was not official until one week before Hayes took office. Added to that was the complication that Inauguration Day fell on a Sunday, so a private ceremony was held the Saturday before. The result was that for one day, the nation actually had two presidents at the same time.

Our heartfelt gratitude is due to the Divine Being who holds in His hands the destinies of nations for the continued bestowal during the last year of countless blessings upon our country.
—Second Annual Message, December 2, 1878

Once in office, Hayes showed himself to be a man of reform and dignity. He announced that contrary to popular beliefs, his cabinet appointments would be made only on merit and not political consideration. In fact, and to the great shock and dismay of many, one of his choices was formerly a member of the Confederacy. Further, he vowed that he would serve only one term as president. During that one term, Hayes worked as a consensus builder hoping the removal of troops from the South would allow the return of peaceful self-government and rally businessmen and conservatives.

Following his one term, Hayes stepped down as promised and retired to his home in Spiegel Grove, Ohio. He lived in retirement for just over a decade before passing away in 1893.

✳ ✳ HIS FAITH ✳ ✳

The most telling words come from a man when he is either under stress or alone with his thoughts. In his private journal,

Hayes muses on the place of religion and Christianity. He thoughtfully ponders the issue:

> All peoples have some religion. In our day men who cast off the Christian religion show the innate tendency by spending time and effort in Spiritualism. If the God of the Bible is dethroned the goddess of reason is set up. Religion always has been, always will be. Now, the best religion the world has ever had is the religion of Christ. A man or a community adopting it is virtuous, prosperous, and happy. What a great mistake the man makes who goes about to oppose this religion! What a crime, if we may judge of men's acts by their results! Nay, what a great mistake is made by him who does not support the religion of the Bible!
>
> —WEDNESDAY, OCTOBER 15

As a Christian, Hayes made little disguise of his beliefs. Much to the approval of the newly formed Woman's Christian Temperance Union, Hayes forbade the serving of alcohol in the White House, a decision that earned his wife the nickname "Lemonade Lucy."

✶ ✶ FAITH IN ACTION ✶ ✶

How great of a mistake it is for people to reject You, Lord. Everything we have comes from You. We give You the praise, not just for what You do, but for who You are. Forgive us for the times when we make the mistake of taking for granted Your blessings and guidance. Let each of our days be lived in humility and love before You. Amen.

JAMES A. GARFIELD

Born: November 19, 1831,
in Orange, Ohio

★ ★ ★ ★

PRESIDENT: 1881

James A. Garfield the preacher stands at the pulpit, thundering his message from the Word of God. Those around him are caught up in his passion as his hand gestures in the air for emphasis while his voice proclaims:

> We not only declare our faith in the Christ of the past but in the present, who is alive forever more. Let me urge you to follow Him, not as the Nazarene, the Man of Galilee, the carpenter's son, but as the ever living spiritual person, full of love and compassion, who will stand by you in life and death and eternity.
>
> —SERMON PREACHED BY REV. JAMES A. GARFIELD
> BEFORE RUNNING FOR PRESIDENT

★ ★ HIS LIFE ★ ★

James A. Garfield was the last of the so-called "log-cabin presidents" who were born on the frontier and worked their way up from the ranks of unskilled labor. In his early life, Garfield was not what one might expect a future president to be. He drove canal boats on a river and saved money for college, after which he became a teacher.

During that time on the canal, Garfield experienced a spectacular conversion to Christianity. His experience and zeal would later prompt him to enter Geauga Seminary in 1849 and become a minister. He traveled preaching several revival messages. A man of many talents, in 1856 he returned to his alma mater to teach and within a year became college president.

✷ ✷ HIS LEGACY ✷ ✷

Garfield was also part of a succession of presidents that hailed from the state of Ohio. In fact, Ohio played a key role in the political climate of the time. Because the political division of the country meant that sixteen states would almost automatically vote Republican and fourteen would vote Democrat, results for the next few elections were almost predetermined by what a few key states would do. Ohio, one of six "swing" states, was crucial in electing the president. Thus, the best way to ensure the support of those states was to select a candidate from one of those states. Added to this confusing mix were new and unique political party divisions calling themselves the "stalwarts," "mugwumps," and "half-breeds." Each had their pet issues.

My dear brother, the cause in which we are engaged must take the world. It fills my soul when I reflect upon the light, joy and love of the ancient gospel.
—In a letter written to a friend
after preaching his first sermon

Another president who had won fame as a military leader, Garfield rose as high as major general, in part because of his successes against the Confederate army in Kentucky. He was persuaded by then President Lincoln to serve in Congress and was reelected for a total of eighteen years service.

In both his personal and professional life, Garfield had achieved great landmarks, and his term as president was no exception. At the time he was elected to the presidency, he was both a senator-elect *and* a member of the House of Representatives. Thus, he technically held three of the country's most significant offices at the same time! In addition, James Garfield was the first president to use his language skills to run a bilingual campaign in both English and German. Interestingly enough, Garfield was also the country's first left-handed president.

As president, Garfield was on a mission to reassert the supremacy of the executive branch. He felt that political infighting and minor scandal had damaged the power of the president. When it came time to nominate officials to fill various positions, he presented some of the most controversial choices. When the Congress tried to block his choices, he withdrew from consideration all the nominations except for the contested choices. To counteract Garfield's actions, the two members of Congress who most strongly opposed the president's choices resigned in protest. Each was confident that his home state's legislature would reelect them and thus force the president to do what they wanted. But their plan backfired on them. The legislatures elected two other people in their place, and Garfield secured his nominations.

Sadly, it was that high-handed but principled style that, in part, would take Garfield's life. As he attempted to board a train in early July, Garfield was shot by a frustrated attorney who had been denied a nomination for a consular post. Alexander Graham Bell rushed to the aid of the president with a device he hoped would help find the bullet, but it was to no avail. Although James Garfield seemed to recuperate well at first, he died while staying at his New Jersey seashore cottage on September 19, 1881.

✶ ✶ HIS FAITH ✶ ✶

ℱew presidents have been as accomplished as James Garfield. Yet, as he stood on stage in the light breeze and sunshine of a fine spring day, those accomplishments were not on his mind. His focus was on the Source of his guidance. He would listen to those around him, but he would rely on God as the ultimate Source of wisdom.

> I shall greatly rely upon the wisdom and patriotism of Congress and of those who may share with me the responsibilities and duties of administration, and, above all, upon our efforts to promote the welfare of this great people and their Government. I reverently invoke the support and blessings of Almighty God.
> —INAUGURAL ADDRESS, MARCH 4, 1881

✶ ✶ FAITH IN ACTION ✶ ✶

Lord Jesus, we proclaim our faith in You, Your life, death, and resurrection! We know, without a doubt, that You wait to usher us into all eternity if we will just believe in You. Thank You for making the way for us to come into heaven, and let us live with that knowledge reflected in our daily lives. Amen.

CHESTER A. ARTHUR

Born: October 5, 1829,
in Fairfield, Vermont

☆ ☆ ☆ ☆

PRESIDENT: 1881–1885

*I*n his first address after President Garfield's death, Chester A. Arthur struggles with how to help the nation come to grips with the loss of a leader. Knowing how pious the former president was, he asserts what is true: that God directs the paths of men and nations. So he makes it very clear that everything is right for those who trust:

> Its harvests have been plenteous; its varied industries have thriven; the health of its people has been preserved; it has maintained with foreign governments the undisturbed relations of amity and peace. For these manifestations of His favor we owe to Him who holds our destiny in His hands the tribute of our grateful devotion.
> —FIRST ANNUAL MESSAGE, DECEMBER 6, 1881

☆ ☆ HIS LIFE ☆ ☆

*A*rthur's father was an Irish immigrant who changed careers from being a teacher to being a Baptist preacher. Chester A. Arthur began attending college at age fifteen and, by 1848, had completed his schooling and took to studying law at home.

Six years later after apprenticing with a New York firm, he passed the bar exam and would later open his own firm. During that period he worked as a teacher in Vermont and eventually as school principal of an academy in New York. His election to the vice presidency was actually a concession to a stubborn faction of Republicans that wanted to nominate Ulysses S. Grant for a third term over James Garfield. That stubborn faction was called the Stalwarts, and when Garfield was shot, his assassin's words were that a Stalwart (Arthur) was now the president.

✶ ✶ HIS LEGACY ✶ ✶

Some have labeled Chester A. Arthur as one of the "forgotten presidents." Although he came into the presidency in a less-than-ideal way, Arthur was one of the few to escape from the White House with more dignity and respect than when he went into it. While some of his taxation policies were hotly debated, Arthur took great pains to keep himself above and away from party disputes. This failure to "engage" helped Arthur avoid many squabbles and earned him respect across the board. Added to that was his very dignified mannerism and impeccable appearance—all in all a relatively good package. Now, Arthur had a little secret that made his tenure as president all the more remarkable. A year into his term, Arthur was diagnosed with a fatal kidney disease, yet he persevered, even to the point of considering reelection.

While his professional life may not have provided a perfect pedigree for the presidency, it did show an inkling of his character. Trained as a lawyer, Arthur was appointed to government service rather than elected. As a man and as a president, Arthur was incredibly honest and above the "system" of dishonesty that pervaded life and government. As a presidential appointee under Grant, he made it a point to root out the corruption in the Customs House where he held office. Although he did tend to retain too many employees out of loyalty when he became president through Garfield's death, many in government cringed at the new level of honesty they knew would be forthcoming.

To that mysterious exercise of His will which has taken from us the loved and illustrious citizen who was but lately the head of the nation we bow in sorrow and submission.

—*First Annual Message, December 6, 1881*

As with many past leaders, Arthur ended his term on a less than satisfying political note. Against his party's advice, Arthur felt strongly that a huge tax surplus was an embarrassment to the government. When he tried to lower tariffs to provide relief, Congress reacted by increasing the other tariffs. Walking the line between party squabbles and striving to bring reform brings respect but rarely popularity or support. As a result of the animosity created in part by such tightrope attempts, Chester A. Arthur did not receive the Republican Party's nod for the next election and was forced to retire after finishing the remainder of Garfield's term. In the end this was a good thing because Arthur died the year after he left office, and his death would have been another hardship for the nation at large.

✴ ✴ HIS FAITH ✴ ✴

Part of Chester Arthur's honesty and ethics came from his Christian upbringing. As the son of a Baptist minister, Arthur was no doubt instructed in the Word early on. Although he switched to the Episcopalian denomination, Arthur did not waiver in what he believed. If we had none of his words or reflections, simply what history tells us of Arthur's life and presidency is enough to conclude that he spent each day trying to walk the narrow path.

A late night dawns in Washington with one window of the president's house aglow. Arthur is reviewing his annual address. An honest man, he is careful to give the praise for the successes where it is due:

> The closing year has been replete with blessings, for which we owe to the Giver of All Good our reverent acknowledgment. For the uninterrupted harmony of our foreign relations, for the decay of sectional animosities, for the exuberance of our harvests and the triumphs of our mining and manufacturing industries, for the prevalence of health, the spread of intelligence, and the conservation of the public credit, for the growth of the country in all the elements of national greatness—for these and countless other blessings we should rejoice and be glad.
> —SECOND ANNUAL MESSAGE,
> DECEMBER 4, 1882

✳ ✳ FAITH IN ACTION ✳ ✳

Lord, in both the times of plenty and in the times of want, let us rely on You. More than riches or fame or success, we strive to be in Your perfect will. At times when we don't understand or simply cannot see Your will, let us trust in Your grace, the same grace that first turned our eyes to You. Amen.

GROVER CLEVELAND

Born: March 18, 1837,
in Caldwell, New Jersey

★ ★ ★ ★

PRESIDENT: 1885–1889
AND 1893–1897

Although many presidents have served two terms con-secutively, Grover Cleveland was the only president to regain the White House without consecutive terms. Cleveland was the twenty-second and twenty-fourth president, which begs the question of whether the United States has had forty-two or forty-three presidents.

★ ★ HIS LIFE ★ ★

In addition to the above election milestone, Cleveland's presidency was another collection of firsts for the Oval Office. In 1886 he became the first president to be married in office when he selected a twenty-one-year-old bride. Above and beyond such peculiarities as naming his favorite rifle "death and destruction" and personally answering the White House phone, Cleveland also had the distinction of being the first president to appear in a photoplay (a precursor of the modern motion picture) called *A Capital Courtship*.

The background of Grover Cleveland makes for interest-ing reading as well. He was originally named Stephen Grover Cleveland and, for an unknown reason, the first name was dropped. In civil service, he was elected mayor of Buffalo, New York, and later governor of the state of New York. Cleveland also had some other positions. As the sheriff for Erie County, New York, Grover Cleveland was also the executioner and had to hang two murderers. While in his second term as president, Cleveland discovered a cancerous growth in his mouth, and rather than add to the country's worries over the economic panic, he had a doctor come out to his fishing boat to remove it. The public would remain in the dark about the reason for Cleveland's little "vacation" until 1917.

✶ ✶ HIS LEGACY ✶ ✶

*A*s president, Cleveland continued his pattern of amusing and perplexing behavior. He greatly expanded the veto as a tool of government by vetoing approximately two-thirds of the bills that Congress sent him. In all, he vetoed more than double the bills than all his predecessors combined. To date, Cleveland ranks second, after FDR, as the president who exercised the most veto power.

Above all, I know there is a Supreme Being who rules the affairs of men and whose goodness and mercy have always followed the American people, and I know He will not turn from us now if we humbly and reverently seek His powerful aid.
—Second Inaugural Address, March 4, 1893

Continuing his predecessor's tradition of honesty, Cleveland strove to be aboveboard. When he campaigned for the 1884 election, an illegitimate child surfaced that had been sired by the unmarried Cleveland. When his campaign managers asked how to handle this revelation, Cleveland responded by saying, "Above all, tell the truth." Partly due to his upbringing as one of nine children born to a Presbyterian minister, Cleveland remained an upright and honest president.

Initially unpopular because of a strong anticorruption platform, he cared little for popularity and was elected in 1884 by a mere quarter of a percent of the total vote. It was his strong convictions that made him unpopular with his party. Cleveland countered that lack of popularity by asserting, "What's the point of being elected…unless you stand for something." The policies that Cleveland enacted, in part because of this belief, cost him the nomination in the next election.

When it came time for the 1888 election, Cleveland lost to Benjamin Harrison. That term *lost* is not quite accurate, however, because Cleveland actually received more popular votes than Harrison. The Electoral College breakdown, however, gave his opponent the win. Never one to retreat in defeat, Cleveland would rally in 1892 to regain the office from Harrison. Such was the country's good fortune because during that second term, he was faced with an economic depression that he addressed through a series of measures aimed at fixing the problems, not just providing relief from them. Head-on solutions like those were what the country needed. When he dealt with both England and striking railroad workers with an iron fist, those tactics served to increase public respect. Unfortunately, this approach was not popular with the Democratic Party, who abandoned the president in 1896. Cleveland retired to Princeton, New Jersey, where he undoubtedly kept up an interesting and unique life characteristic of his past and presidency until his death in 1908.

✷ ✷ HIS FAITH ✷ ✷

Grover Cleveland was a large and imposing figure, but even he was dwarfed by the six-hundred-foot newly constructed Washington Monument that cast a shadow from behind. With the sun streaming in from behind the looming monument, he uttered these words:

> And let us not trust to human effort alone, but humbly acknowledging the power and goodness of Almighty God, who presides over the destiny of nations, and who has at all times been revealed in our country's history, let us invoke His aid and His blessings upon our labors.
> —FIRST INAUGURAL ADDRESS, MARCH 4, 1885

✷ ✷ FAITH IN ACTION ✷ ✷

God, give us the courage and faith as Christians to take a stand against what we know is wrong. Give us wisdom and discernment when it comes to political action within our nation that openly defies Your Word. May we find favor with You and man as we stand for Your truth and confront the decline in morality within our nation. Amen.

BENJAMIN HARRISON

Born: August 20, 1833, in North Bend, Ohio

★ ★ ★ ★

PRESIDENT: 1889–1893

*H*umility is hard to learn and even harder to practice. It is much easier to take credit for someone else's efforts and pretend it is the result of your hard work. Had the president stood up and said that America was great because of what she had done, few would have been surprised. Harrison called the nation's attention to God as the Source of its blessings:

> God has placed upon our head a diadem and has laid at our feet power and wealth beyond definition or calculation. But we must not forget that we take up these gifts upon the condition that justice and mercy shall hold the reins of power and that the upward avenues of hope shall be free to all the people.
> —INAUGURAL ADDRESS, MARCH 4, 1889

★ ★ HIS LIFE ★ ★

*B*enjamin Harrison had a rich, political heritage. As the grandson of the ninth president, William Henry Harrison, Benjamin Harrison was groomed for a life of politics. While in college Harrison mastered the sciences and languages while participating in extracurricular school and church activities. It was actually his study in science that introduced him to his wife, who was both a fellow student and the daughter of one of his instructors. After college, Harrison was torn between a career as a pastor in the Presbyterian Church and a lawyer. He eventually studied law and moved back to the family estate when his father was elected to Congress. At first, Benjamin heeded his father's advice to avoid politics and ran a moderately successful law practice until the Civil War broke out. In the long run, however, Harrison joined the Republican Party, breaking political ideology with his family and his father, who was a Whig Congressman.

Harrison was active in his church as an elder. In fact, church history recorded that he was an usher the Sunday before he became president and the Sunday after as well.

✳ ✳ HIS LEGACY ✳ ✳

Although quite short in stature, Harrison earned a reputation for intelligence in both a solid education and strong showing as a lawyer in Indiana. Serving in the Senate after losing a bid for governor of Indiana, he applied his leadership qualities to politics. Combined with service as an infantry colonel in the Civil War, Harrison's campaign résumé was relatively typical but impressive.

Elected by a minority of the popular vote but a majority of the electoral vote, Benjamin Harrison wrestled control of the presidency away from Cleveland only to lose four years later. Harrison's term saw one of the biggest milestones in American history: the achievement of a billion-dollar peacetime appropriations package.

If I were to select a watchword that I would have every young man write above his door and on his heart, it would be that good word "Fidelity." I know of no better. The man who meets every obligation to the family, to society, to the State, to his country, and his God, to the very best measure of his strength and ability, cannot fail…
— *October 8, 1890, at a banquet of Phi Delta Theta fraternity at Knox College; Harrison had been a member during his college years*

During his term, Harrison's political battles resembled that of his predecessor. The fight to lower the tariffs and to help enhance businesses was a contentious one. Unfortunately, this attempt to stimulate the economy backfired, and by the end of his term, the treasury surplus created by the high tariffs had evaporated. The stage had been set for the economic slowdown that Cleveland would have to face upon his reelection. He was yet another president who experienced political fallout due to a failing economy.

In part because of economic pressures and in part because of the reputation of his adversary, Harrison was not reelected. Upon his return to private life in Indianapolis, Harrison remarried and lived the next five years in retirement.

✲ ✲ HIS FAITH ✲ ✲

With the sun setting and dusk settling in on a brisk fall day, Harrison is penning a speech. Not touting his own merits, he turns the audience's attention toward his Father. With a stroke of the quill, he scratches these words on the parchment:

> Entering thus solemnly into covenant with each other, we may reverently invoke and confidently expect the favor and help of Almighty God—that He will give to me wisdom, strength, and fidelity, and to our people a spirit of fraternity and a love of righteousness and peace.

Harrison's faith was evident in his reaction to the election. After he won, he made a point of ascribing his victory as a gift from Providence, even though doing so made enemies of some members of his political party who felt that they had "delivered" the election. Although he suffered the hardship of a sagging economy and the death of his wife while in office, Harrison did not let that deter him from seeking guidance from God and ascribing the successes to Him.

✯ ✯ FAITH IN ACTION ✯ ✯

All we have comes from You, Father. You are the Giver of everything we have, and we accept Your charge to show mercy to those around us, as You have shown mercy to us through Your Son. We have no doubt that if we are willing to receive it, You will shower us with wisdom. Amen.

WILLIAM McKINLEY

Born: January 29, 1843,
in Niles, Ohio

★ ★ ★ ★

PRESIDENT: 1897–1901

*H*istorians typically mark six elections as key events in the country's history. These elections in part represent a voter shift or a significant change in political power. The election of 1896, which elevated William McKinley to the presidency, was the fourth such key election. Due in part to the tireless work and money of his wealthy friend Marcus Alonzo Hanna, McKinley was able to appear as "the advance agent of prosperity" to a nation hungering for economic stability. That sentiment allowed McKinley to be the first president in over a half-dozen elections to be able to claim a clear majority of the vote.

★ ★ HIS LIFE ★ ★

*W*illiam McKinley was the seventh of eight children born to his family. The McKinleys were principally of Scotch, Irish, and English descent and had worked the Pennsylvania and, later, Ohio regions manufacturing iron. Because of the poor educational system, McKinley's father moved the family to Poland, Ohio, while continuing to work in Niles, Ohio. William McKinley's education eventually progressed to the point where he entered the local semi-nary. He had joined the Methodist Church during a revival meeting when he was ten.

Like most young boys, McKinley spent his childhood fishing, hunting, ice skating, horseback riding, and swimming. His father owned a small iron foundry and instilled in young William a strong work ethic and a respectful attitude. Nancy Allison McKinley, his devoutly religious mother, taught him the value of prayer, courtesy, and honesty in all dealings, which would carry over into his political dealings.

Prior to the presidency, McKinley had envisioned a sedate life. Starting as a teacher in a local school, he experienced a change of life when the Civil War broke out. Enlisting as a private, McKinley was promoted through the ranks, earning the rank of major. Following his discharge from the armed forces, he pursued further schooling, where he obtained a law degree and practiced law in Ohio.

✩ ✩ HIS LEGACY ✩ ✩

Significantly, McKinley was only the second president to preside over the nation as it crossed a century bridge. While possibly unimportant from the standpoint that nothing changed overnight, this new era brought in under McKinley's term would bring radical change for a nation that was, by European standards, barely out of infancy.

Negotiating a seat in the House of Representatives, he eventually achieved a seat on the Ways and Means Committee. Following fourteen years in the House, he emerged as a leader on tariffs, an issue that had plagued the last three administrations.

McKinley's most notable contribution was not on the home front but abroad. Although he valiantly tried to walk a course of neutrality, the public was in an uproar about the conflict facing a small nation and its war for independence against the Spanish on the island of Cuba. Following a decisive three-month war, the United States Navy thrashed the Spanish fleet off the coast of Cuba. Stemming from imperialist sentiment, McKinley worked to annex Guam, Puerto Rico, and the Philippines.

Our earnest prayer is that God will graciously vouchsafe prosperity, happiness, and peace to all our neighbors, and like blessings to all the peoples and powers of earth.
—Speech delivered at the Pan-American Expo, Buffalo, New York, September 5, 1901

After winning election to a second term, McKinley was tragically shot twice by an anarchist while attending the World's Fair of 1901 in Buffalo, New York. McKinley's death was attributed to complications from that gunshot wound. Most tragically was that a new invention being introduced at the fair, the x-ray machine, could have helped the doctors locate the bullets and extract them. McKinley died on September 14, 1901.

✷ ✷ HIS FAITH ✷ ✷

The sky was clear and the weather perfect. The newly invented motion picture camera captured the president's every move as he finished the oath and turned from the north steps of the Capitol to deliver his speech:

I assume the arduous and responsible duties of President of the United States, relying upon the support of my countrymen and invoking the guidance of Almighty God. Our faith teaches that there is no safer reliance than upon the God of our fathers, who has so singularly favored the American people in every national trial, and who will not forsake us so long as we obey His commandments and walk humbly in His footsteps.

—FIRST INAUGURAL ADDRESS, MARCH 4, 1897

McKinley was not lax concerning his spiritual life. As a Methodist, he relied on his spiritual upbringing throughout his life. In fact, when he was shot, his first request was that his bodyguards not hurt the man who shot him. Few have evidenced such brotherly love for their fellow man.

✶ ✶ FAITH IN ACTION ✶ ✶

Father, please forgive us for saying we love You once and then going about our lives as if You never existed. While we may never take an oath of office, we still can repeat our oath of love and devotion to You every day in words and actions. You have promised to guide us for as long as we obey Your Word, and we ask that our daily goal would be to work for Your glory. Amen.

THEODORE ROOSEVELT

*Born: October 27, 1858,
in New York, New York*

★ ★ ★ ★

PRESIDENT: 1901–1909

In looking at presidential history, it seems tragic to realize how many of our presidents have become president by way of their predecessors' death and disease. Theodore Roosevelt, best known as "Teddy," was no exception. Instead of being merely a temporary executive, Teddy Roosevelt worked hard to expand the powers of the executive branch. He took the opinion that unless it was specifically forbidden by the Constitution, his power was virtually unlimited.

★ ★ HIS LIFE ★ ★

*L*ooking at his personal life, Roosevelt resembled more of the Founding Fathers than many past presidents. Born into a wealthy family from the East, he struggled with health afflictions throughout his life. Elected governor of New York as a means of addressing the corruption that was rampant there, Teddy was being groomed for greater office. Two events that formed the attitudes of this "rough rider," a name that stemmed from his service as a colonel in the Spanish-American War, where he served with high distinction, were steeped in tragedy. In 1884, shortly before his vice presidency, both his first wife, Alice Lee Roosevelt, and his mother died on the same day. The resulting depression drove him to a ranch in South Dakota where he spent the next two years on the frontier. In 1886, on a trip to London, he remarried a woman by the name of Edith Carow.

Roosevelt enjoyed the outdoors, and he was crucial in preserving much of our national forests and wildlife. His nickname was loaned to the popular stuffed children's toy known as the "teddy bear." According to Webster's dictionary, the name *teddy bear* was derived from a cartoon depicting the president sparing the life of a bear cub while hunting.

✻ ✻ HIS LEGACY ✻ ✻

An unbelievably active president, Teddy Roosevelt had his hand in just about every area of life. From regulating the monopolies that had formed in the creation of the railroads to earning the Nobel Prize for mediating a dispute between Russia and Japan, Roosevelt was determined to make the biggest impact he could. During his presidency, the construction of the Panama Canal began, and the government began to intervene in business more than it had in previous administrations. Added to that were extreme conservation efforts to improve and preserve the forests of America. He even went so far as to rename the "executive mansion" to the name we know it as today, the White House. Such flamboyance and success coupled with a shrewd sense of political maneuvering all but assured him reelection.

Many are familiar with Roosevelt's adage, "Speak softly and carry a big stick." That maxim, however, really did not apply to his Christian life. He advocated to the reformers of the New Progressive Movement that "of the gospels he wanted to preach...the first was morality."

...in no spirit of boastfulness in our own strength, but with gratitude to the Giver of Good who has blessed us with the conditions which have enabled us to achieve so large a measure of well being and of happiness.

—*Inaugural Address, March 4, 1905*

A man of his word, Roosevelt did not seek another term in office. In 1908, even though the economy was setting the stage for the Great Depression and could use a proactive leader, he stepped down. Since he had been the nation's youngest president to ever hold office, he was still active enough to enjoy travel and African safaris.* Events in 1912, however, made him attempt to take up the mantle of leadership again, but he was unsuccessful. During the campaigning process, he was shot while in Wisconsin and at that time said, "No man has had a happier life than I have led; a happier life in every way." Although he recovered, the above achievements seem to bear that statement out, and they are but a fraction of what could be listed.

✶ ✶ HIS FAITH ✶ ✶

Based on his background and appearance, few might be inclined to consider Teddy Roosevelt a scholar. Yet, the truth

---

* Theodore Roosevelt was the youngest president to ever hold office. Since his elevation to the presidency did not come about from an election, he went directly to the presidency at age forty-two. John F. Kennedy was the youngest president ever elected, but Roosevelt was the youngest to ever hold the office.

he espouses is so fundamental as to be the very cornerstone of everyday life, and the president strongly points that out:

> Every thinking man, when he thinks, realizes that the teachings of the Bible are so interwoven and entwined with our whole civic and social life that it would be literally—I do not mean figuratively, but literally—impossible for us to figure what the loss would be if these teachings were removed. We would lose all the standards by which we now judge both public and private morals; all the standards towards which we, with more or less resolution, strive to raise ourselves.

✴ ✴ FAITH IN ACTION ✴ ✴

Without doubt, blessed is a nation whose God is the Lord God. We thank You, Father, that we live in a land where our past leaders have done more than tolerate You; they have let You lead them. Help our present leaders to continue to follow Your still, small voice when the world's needs and distractions seek to drive You out. May each leader be able to stand in front of this country and say, "In God I trust." Amen.

WILLIAM HOWARD TAFT

Born: September 15, 1857,
in Cincinnati, Ohio

★ ★ ★ ★

PRESIDENT: 1909–1913

As some of the previous presidents had been of slight stature, William Howard Taft went in the other direction. Both large in size and spirit, Taft was Teddy Roosevelt's hand-picked successor. Unfortunately, the result of such close ties is that Taft lived in Roosevelt's shadow, and discussion of achievements during Taft's term was overshadowed by Roosevelt.

★ ★ HIS LIFE ★ ★

Surprisingly, the presidency was never on Taft's to-do list. He was perfectly content to practice law and eventually became a judge. For him, the lifelong goal was a seat on the United States Supreme Court. His wife, Helen Herron Taft, however, had other plans for her husband and urged him to get into politics. Taft was not inclined to run for office, so with the same skills that placed him on the bench, he won a series of appointments detouring through the newly annexed Philippines as chief civil administrator and ultimately as secretary of war for Roosevelt's last term. It was in this capacity that the president and the Republican Party took such a liking to him and decided that he should be the next president.

✶ ✶ HIS LEGACY ✶ ✶

As with presidents before him, Taft had to confront the issue of tariffs. While struggling against the majority of his party, Taft took great pains to reduce the tariffs. Unfortunately, when the bill went to the Senate, they tacked on approximately eight hundred amendments effectively consuming any rate decreases proposed. For Taft, the financial battles were far from over. A proponent of our present graduated income tax scale, Taft also oversaw the implementation of the Sixteenth Amendment, thereby providing funding to all types of social programs. However, with radical change often comes radical disenchantment, and at the end of his term, Taft had alienated many in his party. This rift allowed Taft's mentor, Teddy Roosevelt, to return and try to run for another term in his place. Although Taft secured his party's nomination, the entrance of Roosevelt fractured the party and paved the way for the first Democrat in several years.

I invoke the considerate sympathy and support of my fellow citizens and the aid of the almighty God in the discharge of my duties.
—*Inaugural Address, March 4, 1909*

In spite of Taft's many accomplishments in economics, business relations, and protecting the interior, Taft was one of three candidates who lost in 1912. He retired from office to serve as a professor of law at his alma mater, Yale College. It was from that position that Taft realized his lifelong dream when he was appointed chief justice of the United States, a position he held for the remainder of his life. He considered that appointment to be his greatest achievement even over the presidency. He enjoyed that post for almost a decade before dying in 1930. Taft is the only president to serve in office as president and chief justice.

✯ ✯ HIS FAITH ✯ ✯

Taft continued the legacy of honest and ethical government. He tried to conduct himself morally and with integrity. Although Taft was not a professing Christian, historical record does show that Taft had many discussions about Christianity and spent much of his life searching for spiritual truth.

Lord, please show us Your truths. In a world filled with ambiguity and confusion, we want to know You and see Your Truth revealed. In our moments of doubt, please reassure us, and in our moments of faith, let us share boldly with others. O Lord, You made us, and You know the limits of our faith. We thank You that You never waver, even in the midst of our doubts. Amen.

WOODROW WILSON

Born: December 28, 1856,
in Staunton, Virginia

✦ ✦ ✦ ✦

PRESIDENT: 1913–1921

It is hard to say whether Woodrow Wilson won his first term on his merits or because of the fracture in his opponent's party. Either way, he won by more than a three-to-two majority and was the first Democrat in the twentieth century to hold office.

✦ ✦ HIS LIFE ✦ ✦

Upon winning the election, Wilson summoned the head of the Democratic National Committee and told him that God had blessed him with this position and that he owed no man for that blessing. Needless to say, this too was an unpopular move among his supporters. Sources say that the early Wilson was just as devout as the man who made such a strong statement of faith as president. As the son of a minister, Wilson grew up Presbyterian, and many sources of the time credit Wilson with displaying "Christian love." Certainly he was a man who had developed a strong walk from early childhood. In fact, when once asked in an afterschool club to defend a position he disagreed with for the purpose of debate, a young Wilson declared that such a thing would be too dishonest to do.

A true testament to the sentiment of perseverance, Wilson surprised many with his success. Struggling with a learning disability that hampered his reading, Wilson forced himself to develop a near-photographic memory. This aided him as he pursued a doctorate degree in political science from Johns Hopkins University. After teaching, he parlayed that degree into a stint as president of Princeton University. From there a position as governor of New Jersey awaited him. Instituting a policy of reform in line with the progressive model, he developed the skills that would allow him to be an effective president.

I pray God I may be given the wisdom and the prudence to do my duty in the true spirit of this great people.

—Second Inaugural Address, March 5, 1917

✲ ✲ HIS LEGACY ✲ ✲

The first president since Adams to appear before Congress, Wilson made a point of showing his desire to work with the elected officials, not for or against them. The result of this approach was the passage of several pieces of legislation, one of which addressed the ever-contentious issue of creating tariffs that were successful and did not cause inter-party tension. Another piece of important legislation was an extension of the antitrust policies that actively pursued business monopolies in a regulatory fashion. The result was greater voluntary gentlemen's agreements between business and government and less legal wrangling. While he was content to work within the system on domestic issues, President Wilson took care of foreign affairs almost single-handedly. He often drafted his own diplomatic communications, and, consequently, the State Department was often all but cut out of the loop.

Under Wilson, the nation had to confront a new concept, the idea of total global war. World War I, "The War to End All Wars," became known as merely the first of two global conflicts. Personally preoccupied with his wife's illness and death and a nation who was apathetic to the reality that Europe was in flames, Wilson found it easy to avoid WWI for the first few years. Although he tried valiantly to keep America out of the fight, and even campaigned for reelection as the leader who "kept us out of the war," by 1917, even he was ready to declare war on Germany. With Europe in tatters and American sea traffic at risk from the seemingly ungentlemanly attack of the new German U-boats, the time came for America to wade in with its big club. Ending the conflict by establishing the Fourteen Points for peace and a prototype of the United Nations that America chose not to support, Wilson tried to let the leftover pieces of Europe have defeat and victory without global embarrassment. Almost all of the work to end the war was done by Wilson, although his last term ended just a few short months before the peace process was completed. After his work, Wilson needed time to recuperate from the stroke he suffered while championing the peace process. He retired to his home in the capital where he was nursed back to health by his second wife, Edith Bolling Galt, until his death in 1924.

✯ ✯ HIS FAITH ✯ ✯

As the son of a Presbyterian minister, Wilson's faith in God was firmly planted at a tender age. It was a faith that would sustain him through personal trials, domestic political disputes, and a world war.

Standing in the slowly intensifying drizzle, Wilson would not have been faulted for cutting his speech short. He was a popular candidate and did not need to be out in this weather. Yet he would not sit until he finished what he had to say. With storm clouds threatening on the horizon, Wilson proclaimed:

> America was born a Christian nation. America was born to exemplify that devotion to the elements of righteousness, which are derived from the revelations of Holy Scriptures. Ladies and gentlemen, I have a very simple thing to ask of you. I ask of every man and woman in this audience that, from this night on, they will realize that part of the destiny of America lies in their daily perusal of this great Book of Revelations. That if they would see America free and pure they will make their own spirits free and pure by this baptism of the Holy Scripture.
>
> —Public Speech, 1911

✯ ✯ Faith in Action ✯ ✯

Lord, we are Your people. In a day and age where everything is tolerated, help us remind our country on what ideals it was founded. We are a nation under one God, You, and we ask that You send Your Spirit into this country and into our lives to remind us of that. Give us the wisdom and prudence to do what is right each and every day and to show Your glory in all we do. Amen.

WARREN G. HARDING

Born: November 2, 1865,
in Corsica, Ohio

★ ★ ★ ★

PRESIDENT: 1921–1923

*N*ot content to merely allow his words to be seen as lip service to be dispensed with at the beginning, Harding reiterates his trust in God. Ever the pragmatist, Harding felt no reason to reinvent words that had been so perfectly stated thousands of years before. As he strode to the podium to address the crowd on Inauguration Day, it was not lofty future goals that filled his mind but the words that were from a time long ago:

> I accept my part with single-mindedness of purpose and humility of spirit, and implore the favor and guidance of God in His heaven. With these I am unafraid, and confidently face the future.
>
> I have taken the solemn oath of office on that passage of Holy Writ wherein it is asked: "What doth the Lord require of thee but to do justly, and to love mercy, and to walk humbly with thy God?" This I [pledge] to God and country.
> —INAUGURAL ADDRESS, MARCH 4, 1921

*H*arding's early professional life was quite atypical. Becoming a successful newspaper publisher was not normally the way to become elected to the Oval Office. However, a stint as lieutenant governor in Ohio and a state senator led some to think he might go well beyond Ohio politics. Stepping to the national stage to deliver the Republican nomination of Howard Taft and then stepping into the Senate, Harding was well on his way to earning a compliment that although voiced by an early supporter would be echoed around the nation. The compliment was that he just "looked like a president."

In his personal life, however, Harding struggled in the beginning. In his mid-twenties, Harding struggled to make sense of his place in the world, and following a nervous breakdown, he was admitted to a sanatorium. With parents who were doctors and a sister who was a police officer, it is likely that Harding felt pressured to make something of his life. His energies were channeled into community projects and music. In fact, he once created a bipartisan band that was available for both parties' political rallies. Harding married a divorceé five years his senior, Florence Kling De Wolfe. Florence had one son from her previous marriage, but the Hardings had no children from their marriage.

✴ ✴ HIS LEGACY ✴ ✴

*A*s president, Warren Harding had little time to be truly effective. He did, however, rack up some interesting accolades, including being the first president to be broadcast over the radio. More simply, he was the first president to even own a radio. In addition, Harding was the first president to visit

Canada and Alaska and was the first to ride to his inauguration in the newly devolved "car."

*But with the realization comes the surge of high
resolve, and there is reassurance in belief in the God-
given destiny of our Republic.*
                    —*Inaugural Address, March 4, 1921*

As a former publisher, Harding took a pro-business
stance on domestic politics. In his postwar-depression era
campaign, Harding carried out his campaign promise: "Less
government in business and more business in government."

On foreign issues, Harding supported higher tariffs and
strict regulations for immigrants. World War I had changed
many Americans. No longer the progressive global reformer
or international leader, America retired to a spirit of quiet
contemplation and international distance following World
War I. Warren Harding finalized the peace process begun
by Wilson and believed that America needed a period of rest
and recuperation from her exertions in war. Harding's feelings had a clear mandate from the American people, and he
won the election of 1820 by an impressive 60 percent of the
popular vote.

✲ ✲ HIS FAITH ✲ ✲

Very active in community and church life, Harding served
as a trustee for his church and as a community leader in just
about every charitable organization. A member of the Trin-
ity Baptist Church, Harding was conflicted about how to

interact with his political friends. When word reached this upright president that his friends were using their political offices in questionable ways, Harding would wander the White House corridors during the night. Struggling with depression, Harding was partly battling this issue about his friends when he headed out West on his final trip. Traveling with his secretary of commerce, Herbert Hoover, he died from a heart attack while in California. The country had lost another promising president much too soon. The nation mourned as it looked to Calvin Coolidge for guidance.

Standing in this presence, mindful of the solemnity of this occasion, feeling the emotions which no one may know until he senses the great weight of responsibility for himself, I must utter my belief in the divine inspiration of the founding fathers. Surely there must have been God's intent in the making of this new-world Republic.
—INAUGURAL ADDRESS, MARCH 4, 1921

✻　✯ FAITH IN ACTION ✯　✻

When the world is too much for us to bear, let us turn to You. Everything we confront throughout our life is small for You, God. Let us use You as our Source of strength, not just in the tough times, but always. You created us to walk through life with You, and we are in awe. Amen.

CALVIN COOLIDGE

Born: July 4, 1872,
in Plymouth, Vermont

✦ ✦ ✦ ✦

PRESIDENT: 1923–1929

$\mathcal{S}$tepping in to fill the vacancy left by Harding's untimely death, Calvin Coolidge did quite well for the nation.

✦ ✦ HIS LIFE ✦ ✦

$\mathcal{C}$oolidge was a reserved and terse conversationalist who often related that he would conduct entire conversations by answering only with a *yes* or a *no*. When a young dinner guest bet that she could get the president to say at least three words, his response was a humorous, "You lose." Yet, he would allow himself to be photographed in ridiculous outfits such as Indian war bonnets.

Surprising everybody, Calvin Coolidge called a press conference in a classroom of a South Dakota high school in 1927. He handed a slip of paper to each of the thirty reporters present. The paper simply informed them that he would not be running for president again. Caught off guard, the Republicans chose to nominate Herbert Hoover and let Coolidge finish his term in relative peace. Some sources record that this decision came from a fact that Coolidge, with his small-town desires, felt out of place in a nation where the lifestyle was changing quickly. Calvin Coolidge lived in retirement long enough to see the economy he had helped maintain completely crumble.

✶ ✶ HIS LEGACY ✶ ✶

*H*aving had a strong background in public service, Coolidge was well groomed for the highest office of the land. Trained as a lawyer, he moved into politics early on as the clerk of the courts in Massachusetts where he practiced law. Eventually he served terms in the state and national legislature plus time as the lieutenant governor and governor. Jumping from a career largely comprised of state service, Coolidge succeeded to the vice presidency under Harding. When tapped on the shoulder by the nation, Calvin Coolidge did well enough to not only earn subsequent election to the office on his own merit, but he did so by winning in almost a two-to-one landslide.

The foundations of our society and our government rest so much on the teachings of the Bible that it would be difficult to support them if faith in these teachings would cease to be practically universal in our country.

Coolidge felt that small-town democracy was what the nation's government should embody. This calm, reasoned approach to government sat well with the growing nation that was too caught up with the newly emerging "fun" of life to worry about an ultraconservative leader. In the following election, less than half of the registered voters showed up to vote.

The focus of the Coolidge years was maintaining the status quo of prosperity and contentment. A foreign policy steeped in isolation and tax cuts for the individuals all but assured that Coolidge would strive to protect life as usual. Unfortunately, most Americans' lifestyles would have grave consequences in the near future as spending outpaced earnings. The combination of the overextension of personal credit and other business factors would lead to an economic meltdown. Although Coolidge would strive to fend off the impending disaster, the appetites of the people could not be addressed by legislation alone.

✯ ✯ HIS FAITH ✯ ✯

Following the lead of some of those who had gone before him, Coolidge declared that his victory was the result of God's providence, not man. He gave credit to God for his success, and he lived and governed in a manner that would reflect that gratitude. Coolidge felt so out of place leading a society that was rapidly embracing a nontraditional lifestyle.

Although many of his peers singled out Coolidge for complaining that he was a product of "simpler" times, few men have so embodied the traits of Christianity as he did. Believing that if "in God we trust" was truly the national motto, then the following should be a result:

> No ambition, no temptation, lures her to thought
> of foreign dominions. The legions which she sends
> forth are armed, not with the sword, but with the

Cross. The higher state to which she seeks the allegiance of all mankind is not of human, but of Divine origin. She cherishes no purpose save to merit the favor of Almighty God.

—INAUGURAL ADDRESS, MARCH 4, 1925

✶ ✶ FAITH IN ACTION ✶ ✶

Each day, O Lord, let us go out with Your words on our lips and Your cross in our hands. If we truly trust in You, let us act like it to an unbelieving world. Thank You that You have not separated Yourself from this country even though foolish people in power have denied You. By the very nature of each day, You again show that You are God. Amen.

HERBERT HOOVER

*Born: August 10, 1874,
in West Branch, Iowa*

★ ★ ★ ★

Herbert Hoover understood the fact that the nation's well-being rested upon the spiritual conditions of her citizens.

> Our social and economic system cannot march toward better days unless it is inspired by things of the Spirit. It is here that the higher purposes of individualism must find their sustenance.
> —*AMERICAN INDIVIDUALISM*, "SPIRITUAL GROUNDS"

★ ★ HIS LIFE ★ ★

Herbert Hoover had a hard early life. An orphan before he was even ten years old, Hoover went to live with his uncle in Oregon. In this family of devout Quakers, Hoover was quickly enrolled in the Quaker school that his uncle worked at. He showed an aptitude for studies, and while going to night school and working as an assistant in what we would now call a real estate firm, Hoover was accepted into Stanford University, where he continued to excel. His career was off to a brisk start, and before long he was able to boast that he had circled the globe at least five times. His skill as an engineer and an administrator would come into play in vastly different areas from running the nation to helping evacuate over one hundred thousand Americans from WWI Europe.

A self-made millionaire, Hoover had made his fortune as a mining engineer. Working under Coolidge to transform the Commerce Department into an active and relevant agency, he became known as the "Secretary of Commerce and Under-Secretary of Everything Else." He would carry this attitude and the skills that it forged with him to the White House. The result was that people looked to him to calmly and quickly solve all the nation's problems as if they were one of his mining contracts. Sadly, the problems were bigger than any one man, even if that man was the president of the United States.

✶ ✶ HIS LEGACY ✶ ✶

One actually has to pity Herbert Hoover. Although the case could be made that his position in the Commerce Department should have made him one of the best informed as to the health of the economy, economic theorists today still cannot pinpoint what exactly triggered the stock market crash that led to the Great Depression. Almost as much money was lost in a single session on Wall Street that day than what it cost us to fight all of World War I. For a nation coming off of the Roaring Twenties, it was hard to learn to "live lean."

The programs of Hoover's presidency were unsurprisingly aimed at relieving the Depression. He tried to marshal his talents as an entrepreneur to break the cycle of unemployment and falling demand, hoping for a window whereby reinvestment could begin. Congress responded willingly by passing tax cuts and subsidies at Hoover's request. Nothing worked, and the public turned its frustration toward Washington, demanding action and relief. In spite of this discontent, Hoover made a mark in history when he fed and housed the thousands of protestors that marched to Washington in 1931.

Our strength lies in spiritual concepts. It lies in public sensitivities to evil. Our greatest danger is not from invasion by foreign armies. Our dangers are that we may commit suicide from within by complaisance with evil, or by public tolerance of scandalous behavior.

In retrospect, Herbert Hoover never really stood a chance as president. While no one truly blamed him per se, when it came time for reelection, the American people overwhelmingly decided in favor of the challenger and his programs of aid and decisive solutions. Hoover retired from government service for a short period of time. He was quickly recalled by subsequent presidents and brought his incredible administrative gifts to bear under presidential appointment to chair a committee tasked with reorganizing various governmental departments. He held that position for several years and made significant contributions to the economy. After government service, Hoover turned to writing and lived well into the 1960s when he died at age ninety.

✻ ✻ HIS FAITH ✻ ✻

A brisk murky morning rose to greet Herbert Hoover's big day. With the crowd huddling close for warmth on an unexpectedly frigid day, Hoover represented the hope for a continuation of the "roaring" lifestyle, yet his statements hearkened back to some traditional basics:

> It is a dedication and consecration under God to the highest office in service of our people. I assume this trust in the humility of knowledge that only through the guidance of Almighty Providence can I hope to discharge its ever-increasing burdens.
> —INAUGURAL ADDRESS, MARCH 4, 1929

✵ ✶ FAITH IN ACTION ✶ ✵

Please, God, let us never become numb to this world and its evils. Help us to live in it but never to make it our home. Let us show those around us the error of their ways through our actions, and through Your strength and blessing live an upright life pleasing to You. Amen.

FRANKLIN DELANO ROOSEVELT

Born: January 30, 1882,
in Hyde Park, New York

✫ ✫ ✫ ✫

PRESIDENT: 1933–1945

Franklin Delano Roosevelt leans forward and, in his most fatherly tone, reaches out to the nation through the microphone in front of him. Knowing his nation needs encouragement, Roosevelt offers his words to heaven:

> My fellow Americans: Last night, when I spoke with you about the fall of Rome, I knew at that moment that troops of the United States and our allies were crossing the channel in another and greater operation. It has come to pass with success thus far. And so, in this poignant hour, I ask you to join me in prayer:
>
> Almighty God: Our sons, pride of our nation, this day have set upon a mighty endeavor, a struggle to preserve our Republic, our religion, and our civilization, and to set free a suffering humanity....Some will never return. Embrace these, Father, and receive them, Thy heroic servants, into Thy kingdom....O Lord, give us faith. Give us faith in Thee; faith in our sons; faith in each other; faith in our united crusade. Let not

the keenness of our spirit ever be dulled. Let not the impacts of temporary events, of temporal matters of but fleeting moment, let not these deter us in our unconquerable purpose....With Thy blessing, we shall prevail over the unholy forces of our enemy....Thy will be done, Almighty God. Amen.

—D-DAY PRAYER, JUNE 6, 1944

✯ ✯ HIS LIFE ✯ ✯

Cousin to Theodore Roosevelt, Franklin Delano Roosevelt, or "FDR" as he came to be known, helped a nation regain their faith in democracy.

On St. Patrick's Day in 1905, he married Anna Eleanor Roosevelt, also a distant relative of Theodore Roosevelt. FDR and Eleanor had six children, one of whom died in infancy.

One of the little-known personal facts about FDR is that he was disabled. Suffering a loss of the use of his legs from a late-adulthood bout with polio, FDR would not let that stop him. Knowing that America would never elect a disabled man, he taught himself to "walk" without using his legs. Propping himself up between his strong sons, he would grip their arms and move along with them. Out of respect for him, news reporters and photographers went to great lengths to avoid exposing FDR's disability. Such grit and determination allowed him to govern the country in a time of crisis and be so effective as to win an unprecedented third and fourth term. All the previous presidents had either followed Washington's example of only two terms or had been denied reelection by the people. Never winning by less than three million votes, FDR worked hard for the people, and they responded in kind.

✹ ✹ HIS LEGACY ✹ ✹

President Roosevelt was not just seen by the public as a lifeline on the horizon for a drowning country. To many, he was instead a full-fledged luxury yacht waiting to take them back to the idyllic vacationland they felt they had lost. He won the election of 1932 by a landslide. Although his opponent, Herbert Hoover, knew early on that the election was lost, Hoover felt it necessary to keep campaigning for the sake of the process. There is no way to adequately discuss all of the programs, events, and "firsts" of what is undoubtedly one of the most active presidencies of all time. It would take several pages just to fairly describe a single year of his first term.

In this dedication of a nation we humbly ask the blessing of God. May He protect each and every one of us. May He guide me in the days to come.
—First Inaugural Address, March 4, 1933

Many things contributed to FDR's election and initial success. The perfect chameleon, he could walk into any room or state and instantly be the embodiment of the issues they cherished. Coupled with the public outcry for relief and the widespread feeling that Republican leadership had somehow caused the economic crisis they found themselves in, Roosevelt was well positioned for a win. To top off his appeal, FDR actually had a bold and inspiring plan for recovery—the New Deal program.

This New Deal entailed a series of programs aimed at stimulating the economy and providing jobs by addressing the three Rs: relief, recovery, and reform. One of FDR's first decrees was that no one calling the White House for help would be turned away. FDR believed that if the people had an understanding of the information given to them and faith in the leadership, then it could help create stability in the nation. FDR began his "fireside" radio programs for the American public and held an inordinate number of press briefings. Between the public perception that FDR was working to control the situation and the actual results of some of his programs, Americans began to see the light at the end of the tunnel.

FDR's term saw a surprise attack perpetrated by a cowardly enemy. On December 7, 1941, a day that truly has lived "in infamy" saw the nation blindsided by a devastating attack from the Japanese empire. As with other events of FDR's presidency, just describing that one day, let alone the entire war, could fill a small library. Suffice it to say that America's rally in the face of such destruction and her subsequent defeat of Hitler in Germany and the Japanese in the Pacific were achieved while FDR was at the helm. As both before and since, at the cost of an unbelievable number of young American and Allied servicemen, the grave threats to liberty and freedom were again obliterated. In addition, the war helped end the Great Depression as America's industrial capacities geared up to spit out bombs, tanks, guns, and planes for the war and as such uplift the economy.

Shortly after his reelection to a fourth term and as the war was winding down, FDR was in Georgia. During that visit he suffered a hemorrhage in the brain and died on April 12, 1945. Roosevelt had truly sacrificed his all for the sake of his country.

☆ ☆ HIS FAITH ☆ ☆

*W*ithout question Roosevelt was a man of strong inner strength. Yet one night after his election, he was in bed and remarked to his sons how inadequate he felt in the face of the economic problems of the country. He then remarked that his only solution was to pray, and he asked his sons to do the same. Beyond the grandiose and elaborate statements of faith that others have uttered, the most sincere and simple statements of faith are sometimes the most profound.

> I am afraid I may not have the strength to do this job. After you leave me tonight, Jimmy, I am going to pray.…I hope you will pray for me, too.
> —BILTMORE HOTEL IN NEW YORK, 1932

Heavenly Father, without You, we are weak and worthless. Please be our Source of strength, guidance, and peace. Let us be a light in the darkness to those who are far from You and an example to those who have turned their back. We seek Your wisdom and direction for us, our families, and our nation. Amen.

HARRY S. TRUMAN

*Born: May 8, 1884,
in Lamar, Missouri*

✯ ✯ ✯ ✯

PRESIDENT: 1945–1953

*H*arry Truman came into a doubly bad situation. Kept in near ignorance by FDR and thrust to the forefront during the end of WWII, Truman did an admirable job of playing catch-up while moving at ninety miles an hour. In fact, when asked about the impact of FDR's passing, Truman said that the "moon...stars...and planets had fallen" on him.

✯ ✯ HIS LIFE ✯ ✯

*B*orn in Lamar, Missouri, Harry Truman grew up in Independence, Missouri, and later spent twelve years of his life as a farmer. As the oldest of three children, his parents were reluctant to name him after one of their parents, especially since that could cause family strife. Rather than choose a name, his parents just used an *S* for a middle initial. Truman struggled with poor eyesight during his early years, which made him unable to participate in many childhood activities. Instead, he spent his time learning the piano and reading. Although a fair student, his parents were too poor to send him to college, and his eyesight prevented him from applying to a military academy.

He was, however, able to serve in WWI, where he found

his natural talent for leadership. Following the war he married Elizabeth Virginia "Bess" Wallace, and he opened up a clothing store in Kansas City, Kansas. The marriage was successful and produced a daughter, Margaret; the store, however, was a failure. It was after the failure of their store that Truman turned to Kansas City politics. Truman and Bess were married for over fifty years. She lived to be almost one hundred.

✳ ✳ HIS LEGACY ✳ ✳

While some of Truman's term was difficult for the new president, he did have the added bonus of a salary increase. For the first time ever, the president now made a six-figure income. He was, however, too busy to be long enamored by that as his task was to govern a nation and rebuild Europe while maintaining the domestic economic recovery and ensuring the preservation of peace and freedom throughout the world.

At this moment, I have in my heart a prayer. As I have assumed my heavy duties, I humbly pray, Almighty God, in the words of King Solomon: "Give therefore thy servant an understanding heart to judge thy people, that I may discern between good and bad, for who is able to judge this thy so great a people?" I ask only to be a good and faithful servant of my Lord and my people.
—Address to Congress after FDR's death,
April 16, 1945

Unlike many others who held the office, Truman had made sudden and gigantic strides in his political service. As a local judge, Truman was propelled into the Senate for a decade before elevation to the vice presidency. His military service was in WWI as an artillery officer in France. The contribution that Truman made in the Senate was in fact relatively successful due in part to his chairing an investigation into war expenses—a position that combined his past posts and saved the nation as much as $15 billion.

Truman was faced with some of the most crucial decisions that could have had detrimental results. A new super weapon harnessed the power of the atom. As president, he would be made aware of this new destructive force. After imploring Japan to surrender, he dropped the atom bomb on two Japanese cities: Hiroshima and Nagasaki. That decision unleashed a power that would ignite a cold war that would last for decades. This bombing, however, was not a failure because it ended WWII. In fact, the successful end to the war was one of the successes of the Truman years. As difficult as this decision was to make, he also made the decision to build peace and unity throughout the world. By bringing the United States into the newly formed United Nations, he recognized Woodrow Wilson's stillborn dream of a global governmental community. In addition, NATO and the Berlin Airdrop of 1948 were implemented. Truman further implemented both the Marshall Doctrine and the Truman Plan to ensure peace and stimulate the economy of war-ravaged countries. It was not until the Fair Deal, as it was known, that Truman felt that he had assumed the presidency in his "own right."

From one war to another, Truman had scarcely ended WWII when a struggle began raging in Korea. As with the differences between WWI and WWII, the Korean War represented a new type of war for the nation. After almost two years of being embroiled in that conflict, Truman made the decision not to run for a second term. He lived out the remainder of his years in Independence, Missouri, where he died almost thirty years after leaving office.

✻ ✻ HIS FAITH ✻ ✻

With so much chaos on the home front and abroad, it seemed only fitting that the leader of the free world should turn to a sovereign God to strengthen his faith.

No introduction could do justice to these words. Their soulful cry ring through generations later, and they are still as true today as when Truman uttered them:

> At this...time we should renew our faith in God. We celebrate the hour in which God came to man. It is fitting that we should turn to Him....But there are many others who are away from their homes and their loved ones on this day. Thousands of our boys are on the cold and dreary battlefield of Korea. But all of us—at home, at war, wherever we may be—are within reach of God's love and power. We can all pray. We should all pray.
>
> —LIGHTING THE NATIONAL COMMUNITY CHRISTMAS TREE, DECEMBER 24, 1950

✻ ✻ FAITH IN ACTION ✻ ✻

O Lord, in times of victory let us look to You for our humility and offer thanks for Your provision. In defeat, let us look to You for strength and grace. For those who throughout time have laid down their lives in Your service or in the service of this country we offer thanks. There is no greater privilege than to be a part of America save when we reside in Your kingdom for all eternity. Amen.

DWIGHT D. EISENHOWER

Born: October 14, 1890,
in Denison, Texas

✦ ✦ ✦ ✦

PRESIDENT: 1953–1961

*A*nother of the strong presidents to come out of the war era was Dwight D. Eisenhower. Called "Ike" by the public, he brought the power and prestige of a military hero to the tensions of the Cold War.

✦ ✦ HIS LIFE ✦ ✦

*P*ersonally, there is little to relate about Ike. One of seven children born in Texas and raised in Missouri, he was fiercely loyal. A devout Presbyterian, one can see that loyalty clearly, not just from the words he spoke to the nation during his leadership, but also in the way he conducted himself in public and private life. His parents, David and Ida, actually met at a school operated by the United Brethren Church and made sure that Dwight and his siblings were often exposed to the teachings of God. Ike's father taught weekly Bible studies. Although his parents eventually became Jehovah's Witnesses, Ike remained committed to his traditional upbringing.

A military man all of his life, Ike was the product of a West Point education and a real-world graduate degree in war administration. Although many of his posts were in planning or administration, Ike became a rising star, eventually earning his general's stars and commanding the WWII forces in Africa and France. Following that, Eisenhower's job was to prosecute the war in the Pacific. Although he took a brief hiatus to serve as president of Columbia University, global events brought him back into uniformed service in 1951 as SACEUR (Supreme Allied Commander Europe). It was from this springboard that Ike leaped into the race for president.

Before all else, we seek, upon our common labor as a nation, the blessings of Almighty God. And the hopes in our hearts fashion the deepest prayers of our whole people.
—*Second Inaugural Address, January 21, 1957*

Except for his convalescence after a heart attack suffered at the end of his first term, Ike worked tirelessly for domestic and international peace. In order to help destroy the idea of "second-class citizens" based on race, he desegregated the armed services and continued the desegregation of schools even to the point of sending troops into Little Rock, Arkansas, to enforce court-ordered integration. On the international front, he met often with Russian and world leaders to discuss the threat of nuclear war and offer strategies to encourage disclosure in regard to military issues and thus reduce tensions. While he had the advantage of negotiating from a position of relative strength, the public saw these attempts and reelected Ike by a sweeping margin. Added to that was his efforts to negotiate a truce in Korea that has lasted into the twenty-first century.

Many of the key events that formed the national consciousness of today's America occurred under Ike, particularly the panic and wonder caused by the Russians' success in space with Sputnik and the downing of a U-2 spy plane. Disneyland and a rapidly growing suburban landscape coupled with the surge of what are now classic automobiles characterized the America that Americans just thirty years before would have been hard pressed to imagine. Although he only lived a short while after leaving office, Ike did and saw more than many often appreciate. Justifiably preoccupied with domestic and international peace, he was not against using the threat of attack to achieve a peaceful result. While he cautioned against building military might to the point that it became a hazard to America's way of life, he urged that might was necessary to protect peace.

✫ ✫ HIS FAITH ✫ ✫

It was Eisenhower's farewell address to the nation. Poised for addressing his fellow citizens, he urged all Americans to remain strong in their faith in God:

> You and I—my fellow citizens—need to be strong in our faith that all nations, under God, will reach the goal of peace with justice. May we

be ever unswerving in devotion to principle, confident but humble with power, diligent in pursuit of the Nation's great goals.

To all the peoples of the world, I once more give expression to America's prayerful and continuing aspiration.

We pray that peoples of all faiths, all races, all nations, may have their great human needs satisfied; that those now denied opportunity shall come to enjoy it to the full; that all who yearn for freedom may experience its spiritual blessings; that those who have freedom will understand, also, its heavy responsibilities; that all who are insensitive to the needs of others will learn charity; that the scourges of poverty, disease and ignorance will be made to disappear from the earth, and that, in the goodness of time, all peoples will come to live together in a peace guaranteed by the binding force of mutual respect and love.

—FAREWELL ADDRESS, JANUARY 17, 1961

✫ ✫ FAITH IN ACTION ✫ ✫

Please, Lord, help us to be proud without arrogance, confident without boasting, and trusting without independence. In each area, Lord, please grow us and mold us into the people You have longed to see us become. Let us be receptive and not resistant to that process. Let not our political or preferential leanings distract us from united service to You. Amen.

JOHN
FITZGERALD
KENNEDY

Born: May 29, 1917,
in Brookline, Massachusetts

✯ ✯ ✯ ✯

PRESIDENT: 1961–1963

With the temperature still below 22 degrees Fahrenheit and almost a foot of snow on the ground, many thought the young John F. Kennedy would cancel the inaugural events. However, that did not deter Kennedy. Standing before the assembled on-lookers, this charismatic and dashing leader exhorts the crowd:

> Finally, whether you are citizens of America or citizens of the world, ask of us the same high standards of strength and sacrifice which we ask of you. With a good conscience our only sure reward, with history the final judge of our deeds, let us go forth to lead the land we love, asking His blessing and His help, but knowing that here on earth God's work must truly be our own.
> —INAUGURAL ADDRESS, JANUARY 20, 1961

John F. Kennedy was the youngest president to serve America. Most people who lived through his presidency can remember the answer to the resounding question: "Do you remember where you were the day JFK was shot?" His tragic death rocked a nation and imprinted itself in the minds of a generation and future generations.

✷ ✷ HIS LIFE ✷ ✷

At the time, JFK was the youngest president elected and is the youngest president assassinated. Kennedy, however, lived a full life in his few short years. Born into a wealthy New England family, Kennedy enjoyed a life of privilege but still worked hard to earn a name for himself beyond the family legacy. Joining the navy after college, JFK served his country on the small PT boats of the Pacific. While in combat, his boat rammed a destroyer. To paint a picture, this was a mismatch akin to a car hitting a mountain. Although he himself was injured, Kennedy managed to rescue and help lead survivors away from the wreckage. A few years later Kennedy penned the Pulitzer Prize–winning book *Profiles in Courage*.

Married to a wife who became a national figure in her own right, Jacqueline Lee Bouvier Kennedy, JFK seemed to be the ideal candidate to govern a nation that saw itself at the forefront of everything. JFK and Jackie had two children: Caroline and John F. Kennedy Jr., better known as "John-John."

✷ ✷ HIS LEGACY ✷ ✷

In his time as president, Kennedy was concerned with domestic issues related to race and poverty. Working hard for equality, JFK argued that the nation needed to get back to its founding ideal of human rights, both at home and abroad. Also on the home front, he envisioned broad economic programs aimed at the largest series of expansion since WWII. In all things, JFK strove to make good on his promise to have America move forward again. He was also a tireless champion of the arts and culture. Kennedy's visions on everything from education to economics prompted people to respond with a feeling that the nation was on the right track.

And yet the same revolutionary beliefs for which our
forebears fought are still at issue around the globe—
the belief that the rights of man come not from the
generosity of the state, but from the hand of God.
    —Inaugural Address, January 20, 1961

Internationally, Kennedy's short presidency saw some of the most significant developments ever. Continuing the popular suspicion and loathing of the communists, JFK would confront their "evils" again and again. In October 1962, the nation braced itself as nuclear missiles were positioned just miles off the coast of Florida in Cuba. A showdown between nuclear-armed opponents escalated into the Cuban missile crisis until a naval blockade and some political gamesmanship allowed both nations to disarm the threat without war. The Bay of Pigs and military advisors sent into South Vietnam only served to further increase tensions between the nations.

As all good things must come to an end, tragically for this nation, the end came without warning one morning in Texas. While riding in a motorcade in Dallas on November 22, 1963, Kennedy was shot and killed by an unseen assassin. Much debate and controversy rage over who exactly fired the shot that ended JFK's life, but the man held responsible for it had lain in wait and fired from a window of the Texas Book Depository. The untimely and tragic death of JFK imprinted itself on a nation and left the country shaken and in tears.

✹ ✹ HIS FAITH ✹ ✹

Kennedy lived at the time when a few powerful figures were winning the battle to shift the country's opinion away from God. These few, powerful, and deceived officials chipped away at our Christian heritage tirelessly. For them, America was a people whose rights were man-derived, but for Kennedy there was no question about who really invested us with our inalienable rights.

JFK's religious background was an issue from day one. As an Irish Roman Catholic, Kennedy was able to tap into a vast network of support. However, the nation had never elected a non-Protestant to the highest office. This was not out of any malice per se but simply because a strong, prominent Catholic candidate had not really emerged before Kennedy. As one can imagine, Kennedy was as troubled as the rest of the nation when in 1962 the Supreme Courts enforced a fictionally based separation of church and state and then removed prayer from schools.

✹ ✹ FAITH IN ACTION ✹ ✹

Father, help us to choose to follow You and not mainstream America. As we stand confident in the knowledge that You are God and Your Son is our Savior, help us to speak out against those that would seek to deny or discredit You. If the only standard of our lives is to be our service in Your sight, then we ask that You let our lives be tirelessly pledged in Your service. Amen.

LYNDON BAINES JOHNSON

Born: August 27, 1908, in Johnson City, Texas

★ ★ ★ ★

PRESIDENT: 1963–1969

From JFK to Lyndon B. Johnson, the nation was in for an unexpected change in many ways. Elevated to the White House in the worst possible way, Johnson diligently tried to continue the policies and ideals of the Kennedy era.

★ ★ HIS LIFE ★ ★

As a young boy, Lyndon B. Johnson, or LBJ as he became known, was raised in central Texas near a city that his family helped found, aptly named "Johnson City." Surrounded by the poverty of rural life, he sought to escape but not forget. While Johnson earned a teaching degree and worked with poor Hispanic students, his concern for the disadvantaged and the social underdog flourished. As the nation was recovering from the Depression, he went to the Senate where he became the youngest minority leader. After which, he took over as majority leader when his party regained control. In WWII, Johnson had been decorated with the nation's second highest award for his actions in the Pacific.

*W*hen it came time for reelection, the American voters sent Johnson to the White House in his own right by a landslide. Although personally "unlikable," Johnson provided a sense of leadership that the nation craved. At times crass and overbearing, Johnson showed himself to the American people as one who would continue the policies of the Camelot era. Showing power and energy, LBJ proved to doubters his ability to push bills through Congress and get the job done.

Johnson's goal as a politician raised in the political climate of the New Deal was a "great society" that would take the programs of the New Deal far beyond FDR's wildest imagination. Medicare, Medicaid, education reform, HUD, immigration reform, civil rights, environmental issues, and arts funding were all radically impacted under several pieces of legislation that Johnson supported. These programs were the embodiment of liberalism in a way never before seen. The nation, eager to do anything for the memory of JFK, rallied behind these programs and the government that enacted them.

My fellow countrymen, on this occasion, the oath I have taken before you and before God is not mine alone, but ours together.
—Inaugural Address, January 20, 1965

The 1960s, however, were not the 1930s, and opposition to the price tag of these programs soon mounted. The new counterculture of peace and the free-love movement embodied by a generation of people who are now referred to as the "Hippies" began to take shape. College campuses were in a fervor over the "establishment." The scene was set for a major clash of values, and all that was needed was a reason. Sadly, whatever LBJ's successes or failures, they were all overshadowed by America's participation in a little Southeast Asia country called Vietnam.

Dealing with this conflict that the administration refused to call a "war," although it seemed to be one to the soldiers fighting on the ground in Vietnam, LBJ and his legacy would be overshadowed by events thousands of miles away and the reaction they produced at home. Although the nation had taken great strides at home and in space, social unrest because of race and war tensions took their toll, causing Johnson to withdraw from the campaign of 1968. After leaving office and returning to Texas, Johnson died from a heart attack in 1973, just before the peace talks brought an end to the Vietnam War.

✳ ✳ HIS FAITH ✳ ✳

LBJ's maternal great-grandfather, Reverend George Washington Baines Sr., was one of the most well-known Baptist leaders in Texas. In 1861, Baines Sr., was chosen as the president of Baylor University, a leading Baptist college in Texas.

It was the spiritual influence of LBJ's mother that would affect Johnson's life the most. He discovered that the doctrine of the Disciples of Christ church most reflected his own belief system, and he later became a member of the Christian Church.

Whatever his faults and gruff appearance, Johnson felt the pressures of the presidency. Echoing the profound words of a president long since past, Johnson asserted that the nation's legacy of presidential prayer was a long and full one. Knowing that mere mortals are not equipped for the crushing pressure, he wisely observed:

> The men who have guided the destiny of the United States have found the strength for their tasks by going to their knees.

✱ ✱ FAITH IN ACTION ✱ ✱

We want to thank You for providing us a way to talk to You. Each time we are weak, You make us strong. Each time we need direction, it is found no further than a prayer to You. Forgive us for not approaching You more often, and thank You that You do care about us. Amen.

RICHARD MILHOUS NIXON

Born: January 9, 1913,
in Yorba Linda, California

✫ ✫ ✫ ✫

PRESIDENT: 1969–1974

*R*ichard Nixon is another president whose many positive achievements were overshadowed by a few disastrous events. Public perception of a leader's deception can be unforgiving, as Nixon found out. While it may be easier to begin with Nixon's failures, it is hard to overlook his many successes as president.

✫ ✫ HIS LIFE ✫ ✫

*R*ichard Nixon's family was not a powerful, political family, but they were hard-working people. His father ran a gas station and store in Whittier, California. In school, Nixon had two distinct personalities. While attending Whittier College, he joined school politics and was avid in the campus debates. In law school at Duke University, Nixon forsook those activities and concentrated completely on school, graduating third in his class. He went on to a legal career that included litigation and acting as an advisor to local government. During that time, he also participated in a theater group. It was during one such tryout that he met his future wife, Thelma Catherine Ryan, also known as "Pat." Nixon's original goal of joining the FBI gave way to his working in Washington with the tire rationing section of the Office of Price Administration. It was from that position that he joined the navy. At different times Nixon romanticized his early years as enjoyable but hard, and other times he showed a striking self-doubt in his ability to achieve.

✳ ✳ HIS LEGACY ✳ ✳

Originally vice president under Eisenhower, Nixon had to wait a little while for his time in the Oval Office. After losing to Kennedy, Nixon finally had his chance after eight years. He had advanced quickly from practicing law to one term in each the House and Senate before becoming Eisenhower's running mate. His tenure as president saw advances in economics, stability, and peace. His first priority was pulling our troops out of Vietnam and then healing the rift at home that the conflict had caused. Moving to promote peace on a wider scale, his accomplishments include negotiating peace between Israel, Syria, and Egypt, as well as treaties to address the threat of nuclear war. Economically, he improved China-America diplomatic relations for the first time. Understanding that diplomacy must be fluid, Nixon strove to use America's allies and make peace with her foes to try to avoid a great future catastrophe. Possibly the most viable example of success was Neil Armstrong's "one small step" onto the moon. A vast new frontier lay in wait for mankind, and that had been achieved under Nixon's watch. Reelection was given by a huge percentage.

Unfortunately, it was one single event that would turn Nixon's presidency from the great accomplishment it was well on its way to becoming into a scandal that would enrage a nation. Seeking an advantage over their opponents, the Committee to Re-elect the President (CREEP) used listening devices in the Watergate Hotel. The resulting denials and cover-up would cost many officials their jobs and, in some cases, their freedom.

Nixon was never directly implicated in the spying, but his refusal to turn over tapes that might have had possible bearing on the case looked suspicious and angered Congress. His refusal to submit the tapes and the incriminating contents discovered when they were released caused Congress to vote on impeaching the president. Rather than face the humiliation of being ousted from office, Nixon chose to resign in 1974.

Our destiny offers not the cup of despair, but the chalice of opportunity. So let us seize it, not in fear, but in gladness—and, "riders on the earth together," let us go forward, firm in our faith, steadfast in our purpose, cautious of the dangers; but sustained by our confidence in the will of God and the promise of man.
—First Inaugural Address, January 20, 1969

He lived out the rest of his life making a concerted effort to distance himself from the errors of that incident and successfully showed that the true Nixon was an honorable man who made a series of bad choices. He was a prolific author and died on April 22, 1994.

✳ ✳ HIS FAITH ✳ ✳

As a part of the Quaker denomination, Nixon's mother raised him in an austere environment of simplicity and piety. Nixon and his mother attended services at a Quaker church, a denomination of which his mother's family had been members for over two hundred years. Indeed, the college that Nixon attended, Whittier College, was a Quaker institution.

Many leaders feel that the purpose of their nation is to generate money or keep peace. Nixon felt that the mission of America was to serve God.

> Today, I ask your prayers that in the years ahead I may have God's help in making decisions that are right for America, and I pray for your help so that together we may be worthy of our challenge. Let us pledge together to make these next four years the best four years in America's history, so that on its two hundredth birthday America will be as young and as vital as when it began, and as bright a beacon of hope for all the world. Let us go forward from here confident in hope, strong in our faith in one another, sustained by our faith in God who created us, and striving always to serve His purpose.
>
> —SECOND INAUGURAL ADDRESS,
> JANUARY 20, 1973

✷ ✷ FAITH IN ACTION ✷ ✷

Thank You, God, that You are a God of second chances. Thank You that Your mercies are new every morning. Help us to not take Your mercy for granted, but to embrace it when we face difficult situations. Help us to grow in our faith in You. Help us to make the right choices even if in doing so we become unpopular. Amen.

GERALD R. FORD

Born: July 14, 1913,
in Omaha, Nebraska

✯ ✯ ✯ ✯

PRESIDENT: 1974–1977

Gerald Ford, or "Jerry," as he was known, was something of a surprise to the notion of rule by popular consent. Although a fine president and a strong Christian, he was never elected to the presidency. During the Nixon years, the vice president who ran on the ticket, Spiro Agnew, resigned, and Ford was appointed in his place. Then, when Nixon resigned, Ford became the president. Coming into a time when the confidence in the Oval Office had been eroded by the most significant scandal in American politics up to this time, Ford was left with how to restore credibility to the leadership and lead a nation.

✯ ✯ HIS LIFE ✯ ✯

In his personal life, Ford mixed politics and private life quite frequently. In fact, he was found campaigning for Congress on his wedding day. He married Elizabeth Bloomer, whom many call "Betty." Jerry and Betty have four children: Michael, John, Steven, and Susan. Betty Ford was outspoken about breast cancer, as a breast-cancer survivor, and she helped to establish a substance abuse treatment center that bears her name.

The rest of Ford's personal life sounds like an ad for the All-American family. As a youth, Ford attained the highest achievement in the Boy Scouts and is the only president to have been an Eagle Scout. A star athlete, Ford was offered opportunity to try out for two NFL teams following college, but he went to Yale instead where he was both a coach and a law student. This degree ultimately led him into Congress where he served his entire public service career before heading to the White House. With the exception of his service during WWII, Ford's early career was focused on politics.

✫ ✫ HIS LEGACY ✫ ✫

Funny stories aside, Ford strove to act as a healing balm for the nation. He transformed a reputation for integrity and popularity into credibility as the new president. One of his methods for bringing healing to the nation was to grant Nixon a full pardon and move the country past the Watergate scandal. Ford had his work cut out for him with trying to fight inflation, deal with the Cold War, and work with an opposing party controlling Congress. Ford's policy was summed up by a button with the slogan WIN, which stood for "Whip Inflation Now."

To curb inflation, he used the power of the veto to help business, reduce taxes, and curb the spending of Congress. Ford placed his vice president, Nelson Rockefeller, over a committee that sought to reform the past abuses of the CIA and FBI. He saw success in these measures, and in 1976, he won the nomination of the Republican Party to run for president in his own right. Unfortunately for Gerald Ford, the people selected Jimmy Carter as their next president. The election was lost by a very small margin. Ford spends his retirement days in Palm Springs, California.

Trust in the Lord *with all thine heart; and lean not unto thine own understanding. In all thy ways acknowledge him, and he shall direct thy paths.*

—*Proverbs 3:5–6*

✶ ✶ His Faith ✶ ✶

If there is any doubt as to Ford's beliefs, one only needs to look at the manner in which he conducted himself and his reputation. He was a member of the Episcopalian denomination and was committed to acting as a moral and decent president. He gained in popularity because of his integrity and openness.

He demonstrated that integrity and openness when he chose to fully pardon his predecessor, Richard Nixon.

> I do believe, with all my heart and mind and spirit, that I, not as President but as a humble servant of God, will receive justice without mercy if I fail to show mercy.
>
> —September 8, 1974

Lord, in all things we acknowledge You and ask that You would direct our paths. In the time when we want to turn from Your will, please correct our steps and bring us back to You. In all things, let us trust You, and when others look at us, let them see not our strength or abilities, but let them see You in us. Amen.

JAMES EARL CARTER JR.

Born: October 1, 1924,
in Plains, Georgia

✦ ✦ ✦ ✦

PRESIDENT: 1977–1981

*P*robably more famous to today's readers for his work with Habitat for Humanity and other peace and humanitarian endeavors, James "Jimmy" Carter was also the nation's thirty-ninth president. Carter truly believed that a good man would succeed in Washington solely because he and his ideas were noble.

✦ ✦ HIS LIFE ✦ ✦

*F*ew today know that many of Carter's ideas were formed at an early age. A strong upbringing in the church led him to publicly affirm that he was a born-again Christian. Although he subsequently had a break with some of the administration of the Baptist denomination, he was quite active in his younger days as both a member and a Sunday school teacher. In an interview he asserted that he has taught over 1,700 Bible lessons in his lifetime and has published a book that outlines some of his best lessons. These strong beliefs created the upright and honest man that came into the presidency with the hope of making a difference.

Carter's life after the presidency is possibly more active than during his term. He actively intervenes in world crises and is a strong champion of the Habitat for Humanity building program. He is often seen at a construction site alongside several volunteers with a hammer in hand.

He is married to Rosalynn Smith Carter, and they have three sons and one daughter.

☆ ☆ HIS LEGACY ☆ ☆

*T*rying to truly be a president of the people, Carter tried to make day-to-day decisions seem more down to earth. On Inauguration Day, Carter and his wife walked rather than rode in the presidential limousine. He would carry his own luggage on campaign trips. Instead of creating a spirit of teamwork he had hoped for, some jaded Washington leaders interpreted Carter's goodness as weakness.

We should live our lives as though Christ were coming this afternoon.

—Carter's speech in March 1976

A weakened economy coupled with fluctuating oil prices caused much domestic unrest. Although he made a valiant attempt to ease fears, there was little Carter could effect at home without addressing the source of the problem, namely foreign issues. He brilliantly negotiated a series of Middle East compromises, but his success was thwarted by a revolution in Iran that claimed more than fifty American hostages, which symbolically held the nation hostage. Oil prices continued to fluctuate, and the world watched in interest to see this "superpower" respond. The conclusion to this hostage crisis was that Carter worked on the phone up to the last few hours of his presidency to secure their release. All of these pressures cost Carter his reelection. He desperately wanted his last act to be securing the release of the hostages in Iran. But because the terrorists specifically did not like Carter, they refused to release the hostages until Ronald Reagan took office the next morning.

✶ ✶ HIS FAITH ✶ ✶

Not many public figures would appear on public television and profess faith in God. Yet Jimmy Carter was not afraid to profess the truth:

> I believe, obviously, that Jesus is the Son of God, that He was the promised Messiah. I believe that He was born of the Virgin Mary. Those tenets of my faith are very secure for me....A lot of people who were not anti-Christian thought, when I said I was "born-again," that I had some kind of special visions from God, and that I considered myself to be superior to other people on earth, and that I was going to create a Baptist dictatorship in the White House and things of that kind. Now I think they see that this is a routine part of a Christian's life, to profess faith in Christ....My religious faith is just like breathing for me, and it's hard for me to imagine if I didn't have any religious faith.
>
> —INTERVIEW WITH BOB ABERNATHY, *RELIGION AND ETHICS NEWSWEEKLY*

Thank You, Lord Jesus, for coming to this earth and dying for us. Your sacrifice allows us to live each day in confidence that our eternity has been guaranteed. Let us not be afraid of a world that You have created, and let us not fear any evil that You have already defeated, but in all things look to You as our Provider. Please help us to walk with You each and every day of our lives. Amen.

RONALD REAGAN

*Born: February 6, 1911,
in Tampico, Illinois*

☆ ☆ ☆ ☆

PRESIDENT: 1981–1989

On a June afternoon, tens of thousands lined the street and waited under the blazing sun to say farewell to the fortieth president of the United States. They watched the flag-draped casket of former President Reagan ride by on a horse-driven carriage into "the final sunset of his life" and then waited in long lines to pay their final respects.

In a speech made to the attendees of the annual National Prayer Breakfast, Reagan had proclaimed his faith in God:

> I've always believed that we were, each of us, put here for a reason, that there is…a divine plan for all of us. I know now that whatever days are left to me belong to Him….
>
> Sometimes, it seems we've strayed…from our conviction that standards of right and wrong do exist and must be lived up to. God, the source of our knowledge, has been expelled from the classroom. He gives us His greatest blessing, life, and yet many would condone the taking of innocent life. We expect Him to protect us in a crisis, but turn away from Him too often in our day-to-day living.

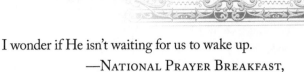

I wonder if He isn't waiting for us to wake up.
—National Prayer Breakfast,
February 4, 1982

✶ ✶ His Life ✶ ✶

Called the "Great Communicator," Reagan was the polished product of his acting career. Acting in over fifty-three films, Reagan was a popular icon who knew how to use words effectively. Exchanging his acting for a place as spokesman for General Electric, Reagan began to drift toward politics. Earning a reputation as an engaging public figure and an affable person, Reagan began to meet and greet the people who would help elect him. He eventually headed into politics as the governor of California and then on to the presidency. Surprisingly, he began life as a Democrat but moved increasingly to the right as years progressed.

Freedom prospers when religion is vibrant and the rule of law under God is acknowledged. When our Founding Fathers passed the first amendment, they sought to protect churches from government interference. They never intended to construct a wall of hostility between government and the concept of religious belief itself.
—Annual Convention of the National Association of Evangelicals, March 8, 1983

Before going to Hollywood in 1937, Reagan was raised in Illinois, where he attended college, playing football and acting. Following college, he took up a career as a sports announcer until a screen test sent him on a wild ride on the silver screen. His fame was not limited to movies; his success on television was noteworthy as well.

✫ ✫ HIS LEGACY ✫ ✫

The presidency of Ronald Reagan has had lasting effects on the nation and the world.

The ultimate patriot and an idealist, Reagan's domestic agenda led the way to lowering taxes, supply-side economics, rebuilding our military, and boosting the job market. He comforted the nation as we mourned the loss of lives aboard the space shuttle *Challenger*. On the international front, his most noteworthy contribution was his steadfast determination to bring the Cold War to an end and the collapse of communism in the former Soviet Union. He was strategic in bringing down the wall that had separated East from West for so long, both symbolically and literally.

Following his years as president, Ronald Reagan stayed on the nation's radar as a public figure. In 2003 the navy commissioned the USS *Ronald Reagan*, a cutting-edge aircraft carrier, in a ceremony in Newport News, Virginia.

Sadly, public appearances declined as Reagan became more debilitated from Alzheimer's disease. On June 5, 2004, Reagan passed away at the age of ninety-three.

✫ ✫ HIS FAITH ✫ ✫

A longtime participant in the Church of Christ, Reagan held tight to his hallmarks—God and family values. His mother, Nelle, a devoted and faithful Christian, taught Reagan at an early age to hold fast to his faith in God. It was this foundation of faith upon which he would build his life, lead his nation, and bring hope to a fractured international community.

As Reagan faced the disease that would slowly steal his life from him and those he loved, the former actor and popular president of the twentieth century displayed his ever-present humility and optimism.

> Let me thank you, the American people, for giving me the great honor of allowing me to serve as your president. When the Lord calls me home, whenever that may be, I will leave with the greatest love for this country of ours, and eternal optimism for its future.

> I now begin the journey that will lead me into the sunset of my life. I know that for America there will always be a bright dawn ahead.

> Thank you, my friends. May God always bless you.

> Sincerely, Ronald Reagan
> —REAGAN'S LETTER ANNOUNCING
> HE HAD ALZHEIMER'S DISEASE,
> NOVEMBER 5, 1994

✯ ✯ FAITH IN ACTION ✯ ✯

Heavenly Father, I know You have set us apart for great things. Even if our goal in life is to bring just one person to a saving knowledge of Your Son, then we have done more than most will ever dream. We thank You that we can serve You and that in You comes complete freedom from sin and death. We repent of the times that we have lost sight of those goals, and we commit every breath from now on to serve You. Amen.

GEORGE
H. W.
BUSH

Born: June 12, 1924,
in Milton, Massachusetts

★ ★ ★ ★

PRESIDENT: 1989–1993

The initials "HW" were added when using George Bush's public name to differentiate from his son George W. Bush, who became the forty-third president of the United States. Regardless, George Bush finally became president after an unsuccessful 1980 bid, after which he spent eight years as Reagan's vice president. Just as Reagan seemed to embody the nation's hopes for a new direction, Bush embodied the hopes that the direction would continue.

★ ★ HIS LIFE ★ ★

Initially George Bush had a very interesting career in government service. He went from a member of Congress to an ambassador to the director of the CIA before serving under Reagan. Before that, Bush was the winner of the Distinguished Flying Cross as a pilot in the navy and, in fact, can be seen on video being rescued by a submarine from his downed airplane. At the time he served, Bush was the youngest pilot in the navy and flew fifty-eight combat missions in the Pacific. His college years were spent at Yale where he was captain of the baseball team. That surely had some bearing on his son's eventual purchase of the major league baseball team the Texas Rangers. Starting in the oil business and following his father's lead into politics, Bush was frustrated by his failure to get elected to the Senate and took a series of appointed positions. Interestingly enough, the 1989 election was not the first time that Bush had "acted" as the president. When Reagan was shot in 1981, Bush assumed some of the duties of the office; however, no formal transfer of power occurred.

☆ ☆ His Legacy ☆ ☆

The Bush years saw some of the most incredible shifts in world power. The Soviet Union finally collapsed, and the Berlin Wall came down. To many the fall of that wall symbolized that the world had finally progressed past an era of fear and danger from nuclear war. As the more dangerous nations of the world tried to flex their muscles, Bush held them well in check. During the Gulf War, George Bush successfully defended the nation of Kuwait from Saddam Hussein and so thoroughly routed the enemy that the ground war ended in a little over one hundred hours. Toward the end of the conflict, the Iraqi soldiers were surrendering to American news crews.

By the grace of God, America won the Cold War.
—State of the Union Address, January 20, 1992

Although that war made his popularity soar, his opponent Bill Clinton, in the 1992 election, campaigned in part arguing that there was an economic slowdown that Bush caused. Although at the time that he announced the slowdown the majority of the evidence showed the economy to be fine, the nation bought the rhetoric and voted against Bush. Added to that dynamic was a relatively new problem, a viable third-party candidate named Ross Perot who was quite successful in fracturing the Republican vote. After the election, George Bush and his wife, Barbara, headed back to Texas where they continued to be active on the national stage and in guiding their sons in politics.

✫ ✫ HIS FAITH ✫ ✫

*I*n his private and public life, George Bush continued to walk in the steps of Christ. He describes one event that changed his life and brought him closer to God to be when he was shot down in the Pacific. He once related in an interview that his goal was to be a man of integrity, to keep his word of honor as sacrosanct, and to truly employ the idea that "your word is your bond." In business dealings and in leading the nation, Bush tried to draw on that principle.

While many point to his son's expressions of faith, it would be wrong to overlook the father's faith. He set his priorities for the nation within the first sixty seconds of his term by telling the assembled crowd:

> My first act as the president is a prayer. I ask you to bow your heads:
>
> Heavenly Father, we bow our heads and thank You for Your love. Accept our thanks for the peace that yields this day and the shared faith that makes its continuance likely. Make us strong to do Your work, willing to heed and hear Your will, and write on our hearts these words: "Use power to help people." For we are given power

not to advance our own purposes, nor to make a great show in the world, nor a name. There is but one just use of power, and it is to serve people. Help us to remember it, Lord. Amen.

—Inaugural Address, January 20, 1989

✵ ✵ Faith in Action ✵ ✵

In the times when we feel that we have nowhere else to turn, thank You, God, that such a feeling is just human frailty, because in reality the last place we turn is the most powerful. Forgive us for using You as a safety net, and help us to come to You sooner instead of trying to tough out life's battles on our own. Thank You for leaders who are still led by Your hand, and we pray Your continued blessing over this nation and those who lead her. Amen.

WILLIAM
JEFFERSON
CLINTON

Born: August 19, 1946,
in Hope, Arkansas

✦ ✦ ✦ ✦

PRESIDENT: 1993–2001

It is hard to judge Bill Clinton's effectiveness as a president because there is a general pallor cast over his presidency by the various scandals that arose during his time in office. Certainly he was elected as America's hope for prosperity and growth. In some ways, he did deliver on that expectation. Just as Nixon's presidency had some strong successes, so too did Clinton's.

✦ ✦ HIS LIFE ✦ ✦

Born just three months after his father died in a car crash, Clinton understandably had a less than an ideal start. Not one to be stopped from excellence, he did quite well in academics, eventually ending up with the distinction as a Rhodes scholar at Oxford University. Along the way, he picked up the saxophone and became good enough to consider a career as a musician. In the end, though, he turned to law school at Yale and returned to Arkansas to enter politics. Moving from a defeat as a state congressman, Clinton became attorney general in 1976. After only two years, he secured the position of governor of Arkansas and held it for four years, only to lose reelection.

He successfully regained the office and held it for several years until he finally went to the Oval Office.

✳ ✳ HIS LEGACY ✳ ✳

Rocked by multiple scandals, Clinton's presidency eroded the nation's confidence in the presidency. Many people felt that his wrong actions were evidence of the moral decline in our nation. Like Nixon, who also made a series of bad choices, Clinton has admirably worked hard to distance himself from his past mistakes. While he has not succeeded in changing the nation's opinion completely, he has taken some responsibility for those actions. Certainly we have all made mistakes and responded poorly. Unfortunately for Clinton, his mistakes were made in the public spotlight. Even before the scandals became public, Clinton met privately with strong men of God like Bill Hybels of Willow Creek Community Church to improve his walk with God. It would behoove each of us to remember Bill Clinton in our prayers as he continues to struggle, like the rest of us, to live the Christ-centered life to which God has called each of us.

James Madison and Thomas Jefferson did not intend to drive a stake in the heart of religion and to drive it out of our public life. What they intended to do was to set up a system so that we could bring religion into our public life and into our private life without any of us telling the other what to do.

—Speech to a group of high school students in Virginia on religious liberty in America, July 12, 1995

𝒟espite Clinton's alleged indiscretions and lack of integrity, no one should reject a repentant heart.

Struggling against mounting allegations, Bill Clinton was in a position where he could no longer keep up the lie. As he looked out toward the assembled audience with shame and remorse in his eyes, he made a request of forgiveness to the people best suited to offer it—the ministers and fellow Christians arrayed in front of him. He looked toward them and offered this plea:

> I ask you to share my prayer that God will search me and know my heart, try me and know my anxious thoughts, see if there is any hurtfulness in me, and lead me toward the life everlasting. I ask that God give me a clean heart, let me walk by faith and not sight.
>
> —National Prayer Breakfast,
> September 11, 1998

Please forgive us for the times when we fail You, God. Help those around us to help uplift us and give us compassion and their forgiveness through the crises. Thank You that in all things the blood of Jesus stands ready to cover over each transgression if we will just ask. For President Clinton as he strives to rebuild his life and follow You, we would ask for Your mighty power of restoration and forgiveness to flow over his life and build him up as a strong instrument for You. Amen.

GEORGE WALKER BUSH

Born: July 6, 1946,
in New Haven, Connecticut

✫ ✫ ✫ ✫

PRESIDENT: 2001–

*A*s this book goes to press, thankfully this chapter is still being written. Although he was the winner of possibly the most contested election in American history, Bush followed in the footsteps of his father to become the nation's forty-third president. He rallied an entire country through some difficult and turbulent times and has made Americans respect the office of the president again.

✫ ✫ HIS LIFE ✫ ✫

*F*rom a young age, the Bush family had a strong faith in God, but it wasn't until the late 1980s that George W. Bush would discover a newfound faith that would change his life even to the point of affecting an entire nation's direction.

Prayer, regular Bible reading, and faith took on a whole new meaning for the future president. Personally, George W. Bush's life resembled much of the path of his father, George H. W. Bush, the nation's forty-first president. Although he was born in Connecticut, George W. Bush grew up in Midland and Houston, Texas. After he received a bachelor's degree from Yale University, he served as an F-102 fighter pilot in the Texas National Guard. He later attended Harvard Business School where he received a master's degree in business administration. He returned to Midland, where he became involved in energy commerce and eventually co-owned the Texas Rangers baseball franchise.

He is married to Laura Bush, and they have twin daughters, Barbara and Jenna.

✯ ✯ HIS LEGACY ✯ ✯

*L*ess than a year after his inauguration, George W. Bush was confronted with one of the most horrific displays of evil this world has ever seen. On September 11, 2001, the nation, and indeed the world, watched with horror as evil fanatics turned planes filled with innocent civilians into flying missiles, forever changing the New York City skyline and scarring the hearts of many Americans. This event reached past New York; it reached out to the Pentagon, to the fields of Pennsylvania, into every firehouse and police station in the world, and into the everyday lives of millions of decent people who had to confront the pain and sorrow caused by these events. George W. Bush appeared as a calm and strong rallying point for the country. We each remember where we were as the twin towers of the World Trade Center came down, and many remember seeing the previously unshakable visage of Dan Rather lost for words and near the edge of tears. And we remember where we were when George W. Bush promised to find and exact retribution on those who would do such a horrible thing. George W. Bush has continued to make good on that promise and has brought a measure of safety back to America.

Events aren't moved by blind change and chance. Behind all of life and all of history, there's a dedication and purpose, set by the hand of a just and faithful God. And that hope will never be shaken.
—National Prayer Breakfast, February 6, 2003

While 9/11 and its aftermath are key points of George W. Bush's presidency, there is more. Instituting tax cuts to help American families and businesses recover from the economic slowdown of the last few years and pushing through legislation to strengthen family values have been key events of this presidency.

As president, he has enacted several tax reform measures and other policies aimed at stimulating the economy. These policies have slowly but surely worked to bring back a measure of economic confidence. In addition, his administration has sought to partner government and faith-based initiatives to continue to help those in need.

A renewed dedication that America continue to be that beacon on a hill lighting the way of the world has been engrained in the everyday decisions of this administration. He has done so with conviction and decisive action, offering the nation the strong leadership it needs.

✷ ✷ HIS FAITH ✷ ✷

As the previous chapters have shown, each president lived out their Christian life in various mixes of private devotion and public declaration. While there is nothing wrong with a leader who is a Christian yet is publicly reserved, George Bush is the living example that a bold proclamation of faith can withstand the public scrutiny. As a leader who more than merely publicly acknowledges his dependence of God but in fact proclaims that dependence, Bush offers future presidents a vivid role model that dates back to men such as Washington, Lincoln, and Eisenhower. Just from his public words, there is little doubt of where George Bush goes for wisdom and strength. Even more telling, the missionary Arthur Blessitt describes a heartfelt conversion experience in which he led a young George W. Bush to Christ as a young man.

It was perhaps the darkest day in our nation's history. The television camera panned to somber-looking men and women crammed into the National Cathedral. Here and there, they dab at their eyes and occasionally stifle a sob. So many good lives were snuffed out in one day that the sorrow was almost palatable. As George W. Bush strode up to the podium, he wrestled with how to bring comfort to a wounded nation. Relying on his upbringing and beliefs, he reached toward the crowd with these words of hope:

> God's signs are not always the ones we look for.
> We learn in tragedy that His purposes are not always our own. Yet the prayers of private suffering,
> whether in our homes or in this great cathedral,
> are known and heard, and understood.
>
> There are prayers that help us last through the day, or endure the night. There are prayers of friends and strangers, that give us strength for the journey. And there are prayers that yield our will to a will greater than our own.

This world He created is of moral design. Grief and tragedy and hatred are only for a time. Goodness, remembrance, and love have no end. And the Lord of life holds all who die, and all who mourn....

America is a nation full of good fortune, with so much to be grateful for. But we are not spared from suffering. In every generation, the world has produced enemies of human freedom. They have attacked America, because we are freedom's home and defender. And the commitment of our fathers is now the calling of our time.

On this national day of prayer and remembrance, we ask almighty God to watch over our nation, and grant us patience and resolve in all that is to come. We pray that He will comfort and console those who now walk in sorrow. We thank Him for each life we now must mourn, and the promise of a life to come.

As we have been assured, neither death nor life, nor angels nor principalities nor powers, nor things present nor things to come, nor height nor depth, can separate us from God's love. May He bless the souls of the departed. May He comfort our own. And may He always guide our country.

God bless America.

—National Day of Prayer
and Remembrance, September 14, 2001

May we continue to pray for our president and the nation's leaders as they lead our country into battle against the forces of evil.

✷ ✷ FAITH IN ACTION ✷ ✷

In moments of sorrow, O Lord, we ask that You will give us Your joy. In moments of distress, we pray for Your strength, and in moments of unspeakable tragedy we rest content in Your continued guidance and power. Help us not to let events in this world shake our belief in You, but in all things good and bad let them cause us to look to You. May each and every day be dedicated in thought and action to You, Lord Jesus. As this country embarks on the future we trust in You because what is still unseen and unknown to us has been long ago ordained by You. Amen.

BIBLIOGRAPHY

Books and Encyclopedias

Academic American Encyclopedia. Danbury, CT: Grolier, Inc., 1998.

Alfers, Kenneth G., ed., et al. *Perspectives on America, Vol. 2: Readings in United States History Since 1877.* New York: Forbes, 1997.

Allen, Thomas B. *The Blue and the Gray.* Washington, DC: National Geographic Society (U.S.) Book Division, 1992.

Bailey, Thomas A., and David M. Kennedy. *The American Spirit*, 8th ed., vol 1. Lexington, MA: D. C. Heath & Co., 1994.

Collier's Encyclopedia. New York: P. F. Collier, 1995.

Cousins, Norman. *In God We Trust: The Religious Beliefs and Ideas of the American Founding Fathers.* New York: Harper & Bros., 1958.

Davidson, James, et al. *Nation of Nations: A Narrative History of the American Republic*, 2nd ed. New York: McGraw Hill, 1994.

Ellis, Gwen, ed. *God Bless America: Prayers & Reflections for Our Country.* Grand Rapids, MI: Zondervan Publishing House, 1999.

Encyclopedia Americana. Danbury, CT: Grolier, Inc., 1997.

Flood, Robert. *America: God Shed His Grace on Thee.* Chicago: Moody Publishers, 1975.

Grant, Ulysses S. *Personal Memoirs* (1885), printed in The Great Commanders Series. Princeton, NJ: Collectors Reprints, Inc., 1998.

Hord, Pauline Jones. *Praying for the President.* Memphis, TN: Master Design Ministries, 2003.

Johnson, William J. *George Washington: The Christian.* New York: The Abington Press, 1919.

McKay, John P., et al. *A History of Western Society*, 5th ed. Boston: Houghton Mifflin Company, 1995.

Smith, Duane, ed. *We the People: The Citizen and the Constitution.* Calabasas, CA: Center for Civic Education, 1996.

Spalding, Mathew. *The Founder's Almanac: A Practical Guide.* Washington, DC: The Heritage Foundation, 2002.

Wilson, James Q. *American Government: Institutions and Policies*, 4th ed. Lexington, MA: D. C. Heath & Co., 1989.

Web Sites and Miscellaneous Sources

About.com — www.gotexas.about.com/library/blprayerbreakfasttext .htm

Bartleby — www.bartleby.com

Believer's Bay — www.believersbay.com/archives/art/01/faithofourfathers .htm

Carter Library — www.jimmycarterlibrary.org

Christian America — www.christianamerica.com

FDR Presidential Library — www.fdrlibrary.marist.edu

First Christian Church — www.dixonil.com/fcchurch/page4.htm

Ford Library — www.ford.utexas.edu/library

George Bush Library — www.bushlibrary.tamu.edu

Hayes Presidential Library — www.rbhayes.org

Healing Scriptures — www.healingscriptures.com/presidential _thoughts.htm

Home of Heroes — www.homeofheroes.com/presidents

Internet Public Library — www.potus.com

Interview with George H. W. Bush, American Academy of Achievement. June 2, 1995, Williamsburg, Virginia.

Learn USA — www.learn-usa.com/q-wv.htm

Nixon Foundation — www.nixonfoundation.org

Office of the Press Secretary for the President of the United States — www.whitehouse.gov/news/releases

Ohio History — www.ohiohistory.org

Praying for the President — www.prayingforthepresident.com/quotes .shtml

Public Broadcasting Society — www.pbs.org

Quotes Exchange — www.att.net/~quotesexchange/ronaldreagan.html

Teach-At-Home — www.teach-at-home.com/fastfacts/presidents/ by_vp.asp

The Avalon Project at Yale Law School — www.yale.edu/lawweb/avalon

Truman Presidential Library — www.trumanlibrary.org

University of California (Santa Barbara) — www.polsci.ucsb.edu/projects/ presproject

University of Oklahoma Law Center — www.law.ou.edu

University of San Diego (online biographies) — http://marian.sandiego .edu

University of Texas — www.reagan.utexas.edu

White House Official Site — www.whitehouse.gov

www.geocities.com/peterroberts.geo/relig-politics

www.mindspring.com/~braniff/inaug.html

www.quotationspage.com

Strang Communications, the publisher of both Charisma House and *Charisma* magazine, wants to give you a FREE SUBSCRIPTION to our award-winning magazine.

Since its inception in 1975, *Charisma* magazine has helped thousands of Christians stay connected with what God is doing worldwide.

Within its pages you will discover in-depth reports and the latest news from a Christian perspective, biblical health tips, global events in the body of Christ, personality profiles, and so much more. Join the family of *Charisma* readers who enjoy feeding their spirit each month with miracle-filled testimonies and inspiring articles that bring clarity, provoke prayer, and demand answers.

To claim your **3 free issues** of *Charisma,* send your name and address to: Charisma 3 Free Issue Offer, 600 Rinehart Road, Lake Mary, FL 32746. Or you may call 1-800-829-3346 and ask for Offer # 93FREE. This offer is only valid in the USA.

---

www.charismamag.com